Brave New
Digital
Classroom

Brave New
Digital
Classroom

Technology and
Foreign Language
Learning

Robert J. Blake

Foreword by Dorothy M. Chun

Georgetown University Press ¤ Washington, D.C.

Georgetown University Press, Washington, D.C.   www.press.georgetown.edu
© 2008 by Georgetown University Press. All rights reserved. No part of this book may be reproduced or utilized in any form or by any means, electronic or mechanical, including photocopying and recording, or by any information storage and retrieval system, without permission in writing from the publisher.

Library of Congress Cataloging-in-Publication Data

Blake, Robert J.
   Brave new digital classroom : technology and foreign language learning / Robert J. Blake ; foreword by Dorothy M. Chun.
      p. cm.
   Includes bibliographical references and index.
   ISBN 978-1-58901-212-7 (alk. paper)
   1. Educational technology.   2. Computer-assisted instruction.   3. Language and languages—Study and teaching—Technological innovations.   I. Title.
   LB1028.3.B567 2008
   418.00285—dc22
                          2007052149

∞ This book is printed on acid-free paper meeting the requirements of the American National Standard for Permanence in Paper for Printed Library Materials.

15 14 13 12 11 10   9 8 7 6 5 4 3 2 $27

                                                    OCLC
Printed in the United States of America   185095576

To Elizabeth, James, and Ian, with love

Contents

Illustrations

Tables

Figures

Foreword

In the twenty-first century, technology is a part of nearly every aspect of life, and this is true of the field of second language learning and teaching. For several decades technically savvy teachers have been using technology with their language students, and research has been conducted on the effectiveness of using technology for language education. However, what is very much needed is a book that succinctly summarizes the pertinent research and underlying rationale and provides some concrete examples of best practices for the majority of language professionals who are just beginning to incorporate technology into their teaching. Robert Blake's book fills this need perfectly.

The book is written in a very user-friendly style and succeeds in conveying several very important points: that technology is not a methodology, that underlying principles of second language acquisition (SLA) must form the basis of computer-assisted language learning (CALL), and that the most critical issue is how technology can best be employed in the service of language teaching and learning. It is not a question of whether to use technology because well-designed CALL applications and websites have been shown to be effective, both as supplements to traditional classroom instruction and in distance learning environments. Rather, it is incumbent upon teachers to consider the types of activities that are best done with computers or via the Internet and to incorporate the use of technology into our curricula, whether in conjunction with face-to-face instruction or solely at a distance.

Robert Blake is the ideal person to write such a book: he is not only a highly esteemed SLA and CALL researcher but also one of the premier CALL software/courseware developers, and he is certainly an outstanding teacher. This is evident throughout the book, as he deftly interweaves reports on results of research and descriptions of some of the most successful CALL projects to date. The questions and activities for readers at the end of each chapter are excellent and demonstrate directly the learner-centered pedagogy he espouses. This book is an invaluable reference for experienced researchers and CALL developers, and especially for those with limited experience in teaching with technology or with developing their own CALL materials. This book is ideally suited to teacher training and to graduate level courses on second language pedagogy.

Dorothy M. Chun
University of California, Santa Barbara
Editor, *Language Learning & Technology*

Preface

No language instructor, professor, applied linguist, graduate student, or department chair would deny the importance of using new technologies to enhance the learning environment—and the subject area of foreign languages is no exception. But the rapidly changing parameters of the technological field have made the first-time entry into using technology in service of the foreign-language (FL) curriculum a daunting, if not forbidding, task for many. My intent here is to explain the use of technology for language learning in a straightforward manner by maintaining a dogged focus on the pedagogy, whenever possible, rather than by concentrating on the dizzying array of tools and gadgets that assist us in this endeavor. Accordingly, this book is directed not only to all language teachers—whether from the elementary and secondary schools or the postsecondary level—who consider themselves technological neophytes or troglodytes but still wish to plunge in and plug in but also to experienced computer-assisted language learning (CALL) practitioners who continue to evolve their CALL pedagogy so as to take maximum advantage of these new technologies. Chairs and administrators should also find ample food for thought with respect to revamping the FL curriculum and evaluating those colleagues who work in the CALL field.

I do not advocate the use of new technologies as a mere replacement for equivalent functions that can be done well with more recognizable tools such as pencil and paper or chalk and board. Rather, as the title indicates, I envisage a radical change in language teaching to occur not solely because technology is involved but as the result of teachers' rethinking what they do as they begin to incorporate new technologies into the syllabi along with their respective affordances. Clearly, I am tipping my hat to Jim Cummins's *Brave New Schools: Challenging Cultural Illiteracy through Global Learning Networks* (Cummins and Sayers 1995), which has led the way for so many teaching reforms in the English as a second language (ESL) and second language acquisition (SLA) fields.

Undoubtedly, some of the technological tools reviewed here will have already been surpassed by other innovations by the time this book is published and lands in the hands of the reader: Becoming outdated is a constant worry for those who work in the CALL field. In chapter 1 I analyze this fear as well as other misconceptions surrounding the use of new technologies that persist among some teachers and graduate students, despite the profession's as a whole having reached more sophisticated notions about technology in the postmodern era. Although newer generations of students may not suffer from these misconceptions and worries, many classroom practitioners, young and old, still shy away from using new technologies. Today's graduate preparation rarely includes as a required subject an exploration of the use of technology. My hope is that this text will provide a sound basis for professional training within the context of a single-author publication (although many edited volumes on CALL already exist; see Blake's review 2008). To assist in this endeavor, I place some concepts and terms in italics, and I draw the reader's attention to the glossary at the end of the book.

Without a doubt, the most ubiquitous entry point into new technologies is the Internet, the focus of chapter 2, but discrete CALL programs are still much alive in the field, as reviewed in chapter 3. In chapter 4 I examine computer-mediated communication (CMC), especially synchronous chatting, the most exciting development in the CALL field in the last decade. At the most radical end of the technological-use continuum is the idea of a completely online or virtual language course—distance language learning, the focus of chapter 5. In chapter 6 I close with an in-depth examination of how teachers must change their approach to language education if they wish to take full advantage of the benefits that new technologies can potentially offer.

Woven among these chapters are ample references to CALL research, although the focus of this book is not about how to do research (a worthy goal in itself) but rather how to implement new technologies into the FL curriculum. Teachers should always remember that, in language learning, no particular technology is superior to any other tool; it's all in the way the activities are implemented so as to engage and foster the student's own sense of agency. Equally important for the *Brave New Digital Classroom* is the constant reflection on intercultural themes. Too often our colleagues from other disciplines forget that the language profession is charged with imparting much more than just the forms of the pluperfect subjunctive in the second language (L2): We all want students to discover and rediscover a new place along the bilingual continuum, a construct that includes cultural competence at its very heart.

Above all else, the language profession must move beyond a simple computer functional competence (knowing how to use the tools) toward both a critical competence (realizing what the tools are good for) and then, finally, to a rhetorical competence (understanding how these tools will help transform the learning environment). The word "rhetoric" normally implies skill in the effective use of speech. But in this case it refers to skill in the effective use of technology in service of learning a foreign language. This new rhetoric requires both students and teachers to put into action a new way of viewing the world mediated by a new language and a new technologically assisted learning environment.

I wish to thank all the technological mentors who have patiently helped me along the way: most of all, María Victoria González Pagani, who showed me what content-based teaching supported by new technologies was all about. I owe a particular word of thanks to the University of Valladolid, Spain, whose scholarly exchange fellowship sponsored by professor Pilar Celma Valero during the summer of 2006 allowed me to complete the first draft of this book. I thank Gail Grella, my editor at Georgetown University Press, whose constant expert advice and steadfast support encouraged me to finish. I also wish to thank the CALICO membership at large for always supporting each other and making what this language profession should always be: fun!

Chapter 1

SLA, Language Teaching, and Technology

An Overview

WHY TECHNOLOGY IN THE L2 CURRICULUM?

Why should any foreign-language educator or student in the process of learning a second language (L2) have any interest in technology given that L2 learning is such a social, if not face-to-face, process? The answer lies in looking closely at the facts of second language acquisition (SLA) and the resources at hand.

SLA, the process of learning another language other than your mother tongue (L1), is both an intensive and time-consuming activity.[1] After years of experience in training field agents, the Foreign Service Institute (FSI) estimates that anywhere from 700 to 1,320 hours of full-time instruction are needed to reach a level of high fluency (Bialystok and Hakuta 1994, 34). More specifically, the time commitment for learning a Romance language minimally approaches 20 weeks of intensive, full-time study at 30 hours per week, for a grand total of 600 hours, while for other languages, such as Russian and Chinese, the ideal exposure can exceed 44 weeks at 30 hours per week, or 1,320 hours. In stark contrast to these calculations, most university students spend on average only 150 hours per academic year actively studying a second language (10 weeks at 5 hours per week for three quarters = 150 total hours). Upon graduation from college, students of whatever second language just barely reach the FSI's lowest threshold requirements for achieving proficiency, that of the Romance languages. For students studying a non-Romance language at the university level, four years of second language study are not sufficient to obtain functional proficiency, according to these FSI estimates.

1

For those students who began studying a second language in high school and continued at the university level, the picture still does not seem much brighter. Many educators and public figures have expressed dismay that so much university language work appears to be remedial, because much of the material taught was already covered in high school. But in light of the FSI statistics, this is not really the case; it simply takes from four to six years to reach functional proficiency in a second language. Crucial to this L2 processing is the extent and nature of the input received—something all linguists and SLA researchers can agree on, even if their SLA models differ radically (discussed later in this chapter). In any event, university L2 learners, in terms of time on task, do not compare too unfavorably with children learning a first language during the first five years, with phonetic accuracy or accent perhaps being a notable exception (DeKeyser 2000).

How can this realistic, if not sobering, depiction of adult SLA be sped up and made more efficient? Increasing contact with the target language is the most obvious solution. In particular, going to the region(s) where the target language is spoken and immersing oneself in the society and culture clearly remains the preferred but most expensive method of acquiring linguistic competence in another language. However, Davidson (2007, 277) warns that less than 3 percent of our university students go abroad on either academic or internship programs. What happens to the majority of our nation's L2 students who are unable or unwilling to take advantage of study abroad? Most SLA theorists would agree, in some basic formulation of the issues, that formal L2 teaching is often unsuccessful because learners receive impoverished or insufficient input in the target language (Cummins 1998, 19). Technology, then, if used wisely, could play a major role in enhancing L2 learners' contact with the target language, especially in the absence of study abroad. Whether technology fulfills this promise depends on how it is used in the curriculum. The principal focus of this book is to discuss how technology can best be employed in the foreign-language curriculum in order to enhance and enrich the learners' contact with the target language and thereby assist the SLA process.

A few words of caution, however, are in order from the outset. First, technology only provides a set of tools that are, for the most part, methodologically neutral. Selber (2004, 36) has called this attitude toward technology the tool metaphor: "From a functionalist design perspective, good tools become invisible once users understand their basic operation." In reality, all tools mediate our experiences in certain ways, which is to say that they are not totally value free. Applied linguists working within an ecological framework would say that every technology provides certain affordances and therefore is not neutral (Zhao et al. 2005; Levy 2006, 13–15).

Despite this word of caution, how technological tools are used should largely be guided by a particular theoretical model and by those who practice it. In this book I affirm the basic approach to SLA that claims that a second language is best learned and taught through interaction (for a similar endorsement, see Long 1991, and with reference to the computer learning environment, see Chapelle 2001). Pica, Kanagy, and Falodun (1993, 11) represent well the interactionist stance when they state, "Language learning is assisted through social interaction of learners and their interlocutors, particularly *when they negotiate toward mutual comprehension of each other's message meaning*" (emphasis added). The question examined in this book, then, is whether technology can offer the L2 curriculum certain benefits within this theoretical framework, and if so, how these technologically assisted activities should fit in with the FL curriculum.

At first blush this theoretical approach as applied to the field of computer-assisted language learning (CALL) might appear counterintuitive, ironic, or even futile. After all, computers are not human and cannot interact with anyone in the sense that two human beings can. Nevertheless, Reeves and Nass (1996, 5) have convincingly argued the following: "People's interactions with computers, television, and new media are fundamentally social and natural, just like interactions in real life." In their research they found that users are polite to computers and respond to the personality of both the interface and whatever computer agents are present. In other words, computers are social actors as well, at least from the students' perspective, which is all that really matters (28). Reeves and Nass's research further reinforces the notion that computers can make a significant contribution to the SLA process because the students themselves feel that they are interacting with the computer in a real social manner. The question of whether computer-mediated communication is facilitative to the acquisition process will be examined in more depth in chapter 5.

The book's second disclaimer is that this is not a how-to manual: I will not be instructing readers how to get connected to the Internet, how to write home pages in html or JavaScript, or how to program in Macromedia

Director. There are plenty of technical guides or workshops designed to teach these hands-on skills. Rather, this book focuses on why certain technological tools should be integrated into the L2 curriculum and what potential contribution these tools stand to make to any given language program. My objectives are to stimulate the technologically inexperienced readers to go out and acquire the necessary hardware and technical skills to begin incorporating technology into their classrooms. For the language professional who already has some knowledge of technology, I promise to stimulate the imagination for what might be done with computers in the L2 classroom, now and in the near future. All language professionals need to become acquainted with the potential advantages of using technology in their programs. Without some general claims to success and media superiority, chairs, deans, and other decision-making bodies won't understand or support new ways of teaching second languages with technology.

It is misleading to talk about technology as if one were dealing with just a single, homogeneous tool; different technologically based tools render different advantages for L2 learning. For instance, the Internet is an ideal tool for allowing students to gain access to authentic L2 materials; it might be the next best alternative to actually going abroad. L2 students can virtually "travel" to French-speaking Africa, Tokyo, or the Peruvian Incan ruins of Machu Picchu with just a click of the mouse. Non-English pages account for 68 percent of the postings on the web.[2] More important, the web gives all peoples a channel to express their voice, promote their self-image, and legitimize their goals. This sense of authenticity provides endless topics for cross-cultural analysis and discussions in any content-driven classroom.

The advantages for carrying out online discussions via computer have been well documented in the research literature (see chapter 4 on computer-mediated communication). Researchers frequently cite the computer's usefulness as: (a) a text-based medium that amplifies students' attention to linguistic form (Warschauer 1997b); (b) a stimulus for increased written L2 production (Kern 1995); (c) a less stressful environment for L2 practice (Chun 1998); (d) a more equitable and nonthreatening forum for L2 discussions, especially for women, minorities, and nonassertive personalities (Warschauer 1997a, 1997b); and (e) an expanded access channel with possibilities for creating global learning networks (Cummins and Sayers 1995). Swaffar (1998, 1) has summarized the benefits derived from computer-mediated communication (CMC) as compared with classroom oral exchanges: "Networked exchanges seem to help all individuals in language classes engage more frequently, with greater confidence, and with greater enthusiasm in the communicative process than is characteristic for similar students in oral classrooms."

Ironically, telling students that their responses will also be saved by the computer for research purposes (see chapters 4 and 5) does not seem to diminish their level of participation or their sense that the computer affords them a relatively anonymous, or at least protected, environment for their discussions (Pellettieri 2000).

More important, 84 percent of teenagers today, who will be the college language learners of tomorrow, use the Internet primarily as a tool for communications through instant messaging (IM) and text messaging (Lenhart, Madden, and Hitlin 2005). This means that CMC is not only a familiar activity to this new crop of university language learners but also the preferred tool. Members of our profession need to harness these students' disposition to chat online in order to maintain interest in FL learning.

Let us now return for a moment to the educational advantages of increased access to instruction and other learners outside the normal constraints of the classroom via computer. Public schools, in particular, are faced with ever-increasing enrollment pressures, a veritable flood of baby-boomer children reaching college age: the U.S. Department of Education reports that enrollments increased 25 percent to 17.3 million students from 1990 to 2004, and it projects an additional 15 percent increase to 19.9 million students by 2015 (National Center for Educational Statistics 2006). It is doubtful that all of these students, or at least anyone who wants access to higher education, will find seats in a classroom setting as presently configured. Some L2 instruction in the future will have to take place at a distance or through what publishers call the home market. This does not diminish the on-campus/classroom experience; on the contrary, its value will appreciate even more, but access to that privileged learning format might not be available to everyone interested in language study. Likewise, as our nation slowly breaks out of its English-only dream (or nightmare), all kinds of learners will make known their interests in acquiring some type of L2 proficiency, whether to enter the global marketplace or, in the case of highly diversified states such as California or Florida, just to understand and get along better with their neighbors. This new demand will be met by an aggressive response either from our language profession or by the more profit-minded publishing companies, or both. Most language professionals rightly feel that they should take the lead in determining the nature of instruction for this new and potentially significant audience. But will the language profession be ready to meet this challenge? Yes, but only if teachers start experimenting now with ways to enhance SLA through technology.

Many of the examples cited earlier have dealt most closely with the beginning and intermediate levels, the lower-division language curriculum. Why should these courses be of concern to literature professors who typically do not teach language—and sometimes, not even culture in an explicit fashion? If incorporating technology into the curriculum can stimulate—and even improve—the overall language preparation of those majoring in a language, then literature professors also have a vital stake in promoting technology. In reality, all undergraduate courses, whether examining Cervantes's novels, reading French symbolist poetry, or dissecting Chinese cinema, are language courses at their most fundamental level. (Remember that it takes four to six years to develop high oral fluency in a second language, according to the FSI's findings, without considering the additional demands of what is called "advanced literacy" or higher-order L2 reading and L2 writing skills.)[3]

Literature professors are often caught in a dilemma: Their language programs are too weak to prepare their students to read the original texts, but reading them in translation does nothing to further their students' L2 proficiency. The death knell of a foreign-language literature program begins to sound when all of the upper-division courses and their writing assignments are administered in English because the students are unable cope with the more sophisticated forms of literary registers. The blame for this situation must be spread around, and literature professors solely concerned with teaching content bear their share. Pressure from the dean to fill those upper-division courses with students can also be a motivating factor in offering Chinese Poetry in Translation or any other subject. No doubt these courses in translation play an important role for students' general education within the undergraduate curriculum, but if the entire foreign language curriculum switches entirely over to English as the medium of instruction, much will have been lost in the realm of cognitive development and humanities. There are significant cognitive benefits derived from learning a second language. Scholars such as Kramsch (1993) have made it abundantly clear that the process of learning another language involves much more than just skill-acquiring and skill-using faculties. Learning another language also presents an opportunity for a critical interrogation of the very notion of culture, which is an appropriate upper-division activity in the liberal arts context (also see Kramsch and Anderson 1999).

In all fairness, colleagues teaching languages such as Chinese or Japanese, with complex writing systems, justifiably express anxiety and frustration with respect to these upper-division courses. These writing systems impose a steep learning curve above and beyond the normal challenges of achieving oral proficiency. All upper-division language courses critically involve advanced levels of literary proficiency, in addition to oral proficiency, which is not normally achieved by Japanese and Chinese children in their native countries until early adolescence. It is unreasonable to expect university language students to gain advanced literacy in just four, short years without active guidance from their professors. Knowing that these conditions result from the natural parameters imposed by the SLA process should assuage our colleagues' sense of disappointment and deflect the frequent cries of outrage over the issue of remedial language instruction; in other words, in the first four or five years of learning another language, nothing is remedial. Much cognitive progress is happening in these upper-division language courses, even if the content difficulty must be modified for the particular language and students in question.

Less commonly taught languages (LCTLs) often suffer from another curriculum dilemma: the need for quality pedagogical materials at all levels, which typically goes unmet due to low commercial profit margins at the publishing houses. Publishers project small enrollments for these languages and consequently have little motivation to produce print materials for them. Fortunately, new technological advances for web-based courses and CD-ROM applications offer language professionals the opportunity to create their own L2 materials that respond to the specific needs of their students. In short, a strong, technologically modernized language program will always be an advantage to all concerned in the department and will support a healthy major.

In addition, most institutions of higher education are affected by the prevalent student trend to gravitate toward courses that deal with either culture or language rather than literature. By offering an L2 culture course supplemented by art or other forms of culture available in the form of web materials, language departments can recapture student interest. Extended class discussions via e-mail, listservs, or chat programs can further augment student interest as well as student-student and student-instructor interactions. In fact, Gonglewski (1999) has already laid out in clear terms how using technology can satisfy the demands of a curriculum based on the National Standards' (ACTFL 1996) five Cs: communication, cultures, comparisons, connections, and communities.

By the same token, it is important not to raise unrealistic expectations with respect to technology's possible contribution to the L2 curriculum. Negative reactions to the introduction of technology into the L2 classroom feed off the failed promises of the audio-lingual lab of the 1960s. Dashed expectations from that era have created a residual distrust of technology and account for many language teachers' reluctance to plunge into the implementation of any new technologies in the face of few demonstrable results (Roblyer 1988) and even fewer tangible career paybacks (Quinn 1990, 300; Garrett and Liddell 2004). To compound these initial suspicions further, many people have less than a clear notion of what technology means for L2 learning. Unfortunately, misconception about technology and language learning abound; some of these will be discussed in the next section.

FOUR MYTHS ABOUT TECHNOLOGY AND SLA

Four myths or misconceptions readily come to mind when the word *technology* is mentioned in language circles (also see Egbert, Paulus, and Nakamichi 2002; and Lam 2000): In the first place, some language professionals refer to technology as if it were a monolithic concept straight out of Stanley Kubrick's movie *2001: A Space Odyssey*. This myth suggests that technology is either all good or all bad—that is say, all technology is the same. Second, some teachers who are overly enthusiastic about technology subscribe to the misconception that technology itself embodies some new and superior methodological approach to language teaching, although, in truth, all the new digital technologies offer is a new set of tools that can function in service of the language curriculum with the correct application. In other words, how these tools are used and to what principled ends define the scope of a methodology, but the mere use of technology by itself will not improve the curriculum. Third, all of us would like to believe (although we know better) that today's technology is sufficient for tomorrow's challenges. The fact that technology is constantly changing constitutes a frightening barrier for many language professionals who fear that they cannot possibly keep pace with new advances. Finally, the language profession suffers from the fear that technology will replace language teachers. Let's look more carefully at these four barriers to using technology in the FL curriculum.

Technology Is Monolithic

Have you noticed how people use the word *Internet* in an almost mystical fashion? "Ah, the Internet," they say, as if one word says it all. (A few years back, the magical term in our profession was CALL.) There isn't *one* technology best suited for language study, but rather there is an array of technological tools that can be harnessed, efficiently or otherwise, to the ends of learning a second language or studying the SLA process. Moreover, these technological tools change very rapidly.

More specifically, there are three important technological platforms that provide tools to assist language learning, in order of increasing interactivity:[4] the web, CD-ROM or hypermedia applications, and network-based communication (i.e., e-mail, electronic mailing list, user groups, MOOs, chat programs, blogs, and wikis).

The web offers a variety of authentic target-language resources: a virtual trip to Peru, a guided bicycle trip to Santiago de Compostela, and a wine guide for La Rioja, the murals of Orozco, to name only a few examples for Spanish—but materials for Chinese, French, Italian, Japanese, and Russian abound as well, along with an ever-increasingly sophisticated array of web courses and self-tests. Teachers are beginning to use web pages, both original and adapted, to serve as the students' primary source materials, especially in content-based language courses. In this type of course, students work through the tasks and activities laid out before them and only gradually have recourse to learning the grammar (for a technologically supported, content-based approach, see Barson 1991; and Debski 1997). The web pages exist to provide content stimulation and a means for further inquiry. Given the richness of non-English web materials, the class can move in new directions at any point or deepen their knowledge of any particular topic. For the experienced teacher who knows how to take advantage of these obvious communicative opportunities, a web-based, content-driven approach is a dream come true—and the students respond in kind. Something like this type of web-based course might eventually displace the notion of a static textbook, copyright problems notwithstanding. These issues are more fully explored in chapter 2.

The CD-ROM and DVD platforms were designed to deliver specific applications that take advantage of large amounts of sound, graphics, and video files. The publishing industry is increasingly involved in producing high-quality CD-ROMs and DVDs because the marketplace is demanding it.[5] One of the jobs of today's language faculty and lab personnel is to keep track of this new generation of language CD-ROMs and DVDs and to know how to review them, which is a catch-22 in itself: Language professionals need to know something about interface design and computer pedagogy in order to be able to review software in the first place. Teachers must be trained to recognize well-grounded pedagogy when they see it, hear it, and read it on the screen. Many of today's CD-ROMs have sophisticated visual interfaces, but one has to be careful that the medium does not dominate the message, to borrow a phrase from Marshall McLuhan (1964). The benefits offered by these platforms will be more fully examined in chapter 3.

Finally, CMC provides a third platform where L2 students can transcend the spatial and temporal confines of the classroom via the Internet. E-mail or asynchronous (i.e., differed-time) communication and chat or synchronous (i.e., real-time) communication offers students the highest level of interactivity because they permit one-on-one, personal exchanges. SLA research has clearly demonstrated the importance of learning language through face-to-face exchanges that require the learners to negotiate meaning with other learners and/or native speakers (Pica 1994; Long 1981, 1991; Gass 1997; Gass and Varonis 1994; Doughty 1998; Blake 2000, 2005a). When asked to negotiate meaning, L2 students are forced to notice what they do not know and, subsequently, seek a resolution to their linguistic or cultural misunderstanding before resuming the free flow of dialogue. This process of mutual assistance, what many researchers refer to as scaffolding, appears to be one of the principal ways in which students gradually liberate themselves from a seemingly interminable and ever-changing period of interlanguage, the interim stages of a learner's emerging L2 linguistic system, in pursuit of more advanced proficiency in the target language.

Students can carry off these negotiation events during regularly scheduled class time or lab sessions, but the benefits of negotiating meaning can also be obtained through synchronous network-based communication (Pelletieri 2000; Blake 2000). This means that students can engage in negotiating meaning anytime from home or the lab. This use of technology opens the door to an untapped potential for L2 language use. Again, all theorists agree that increasing the amount and quality of the students' L2 input (with output, too, even better) is crucial to SLA success. CMC has an enormous contribution to make to the L2 curriculum, if teachers will become familiar enough with the technology to be able to incorporate it into the students' out-of-class assignments. Chapter 4 discusses this topic in more detail.

Technology Constitutes a Methodology

No SLA theory has anything to say directly about language teaching; the field's principal goals consist of studying the process of how languages are acquired, not how they are taught. Nevertheless, particular teaching methodologies (e.g., total physical response [TPR], the Natural Method, or the communicative classroom) necessarily attempt to make the leap between theory and practice by identifying the most favorable conditions for L2 learning. In an ideal world, then, a methodology should be informed by what is known about the nature of the SLA process:[6] for instance, claims such as "all L2 learning requires comprehensible input, or better yet, intake." Technology, per se, has no stake in any particular theoretical model or teaching methodology: The technology is theoretically and methodologically neutral. But how technology is used—its particular culture of practice—is not neutral; it responds to what the practitioners understand or believe to be true about SLA. Teachers inexperienced in using technology often harbor the belief that merely transforming an activity into a web or CALL format will guarantee its success for students. Again, any activity without adequate pedagogical planning—technologically enhanced or not—will produce unsatisfactory results with students, even if it's attractive from a multimedia point of view (e.g., colors, graphics, photos, video, sound).

Many teachers feel that the only curricular role for technology is to relieve the teacher of the more burdensome aspects of testing and rote drills, so that classroom time can be fully utilized for communication. For example, in the past the Spanish and Italian programs at the University of Illinois have employed a web-based program called Mallard to free up the maximum amount of classroom time for communicative activities and to justify the decrease in the course's seat time requirements from five to three hours a week (for more information and evaluation of Mallard, see Arvan and Musumeci 1999; Echávez-Solano 2003; Epps 2004; Scida and Saury 2006; and Walczynski 2002). The research has shown that there are no significant differences in final grades among the experimental (Mallard) group and the control group, with Scida and Saury's (2006) study registering slightly higher final grades for the group using Mallard. Researchers attributed much of the student success with the Mallard program to the students' ability to continue working on the exercises until reaching 100 percent accuracy. In essence, the availability of the tutorial CALL program appears to have allowed students to dedicate more time to making their control of the basic language structures more automatic.

In practical terms only, programs such as Mallard allow teachers (i.e., teacher's assistants or TAs) to handle more students with the same number of faculty/TA resources. Naturally, the administration is delighted with this increase in the student/teacher ratio. Likewise, some teachers are happy to not have to bother with morphologically based drills and tests during precious class time, which goes against the theoretical bent of the communicative classroom, and the students enjoy increased access for completing the language requirement. This appears to constitute a win-win situation for all concerned and an appropriate use of technology for these programs. Other institutions may wish to explore different solutions, depending on their respective expectations and theoretical orientations.

Today's Technology Is All We Need to Know

Constant change is a frightening phenomenon for most people, but that is the inherent nature of the technology field: New tools are being created all the time. As Hanson-Smith (2006, 301) observes: "One of the most significant problems facing computer-using teachers is that no education curriculum can prepare them for the swift and continuing changes that take place in the world of technology." To cope with the field's intrinsic flux, language programs need long-term institutional support, both from the campus information technology services that are delivered locally in the form of a designated language lab and through a collegewide humanities technology-resource person. It should be patently obvious that technology rarely helps anyone save money. In most cases, it engenders more financial commitment, at least at the beginning. Nevertheless, new technologies allow an institution's human resources to work more efficiently and can provide greater educational access for students, along with offering new channels for learning. New advances in technology allow an institution's personnel to do new things and therefore represent a catalyst for change.

Accordingly, working with technology requires constant updating and continuing education, which can be a very threatening concept for language professionals who are used to concentrating on teaching to established standards (i.e., keeping performance level constant) and achieving dominance of the more literary and prestigious registers of their respective world language. The often-repeated joke holds true for language faculty: "How many professors does it take to change a lightbulb?" The punch line comes from the faculty's own response: "Change?"

In all seriousness, this situation conjures up a natural conflict of interest from which language professionals are not immune. It should come as no surprise that the vertiginous pace of technological changes is responsible for considerable resistance to implementing technology into the L2 curriculum. "Who has the time for that kind of an investment," some teachers might intone. Yet there are other, more powerful fears that stand in the way of using technology: "Will technology replace the teacher or the courses in the department?"

Technology Will Replace Teachers

Put bluntly, some in our profession fear that the use of technology will replace them and the courses they teach, especially when mention is made of completely virtual online courses (i.e., distance language learning; see chapter 6). Their fears are frequently fed by administrators who openly seek budgetary savings through downsizing the extremely labor-intensive language programs. In this mad rush, everyone seems to forget to answer the questions of who will teach those distance learning courses, write the curriculum, and train students to work within this format.

The technology platforms I have mentioned earlier—the web, CD-ROM/DVD, and CMC—do not pose a threat to language professionals but rather complement what can be done in the L2 classroom, if used wisely. Will technology expand in the future from this complementary role to replacing the teacher and the classroom venue completely? A rational response to this question might be that technology will not replace teachers in the future, but rather teachers who use technology will probably replace teachers who do not (Clifford 1987, 13). Again, this implies hiring new faculty with at least a modicum of technological expertise, along with implementing training programs for the existing faculty so that they can come up to speed with new advances. In this context, it is easy to see why many language professionals might eschew the introduction of technology into the L2 curriculum by fiercely adhering to Newton's second law of motion that says that bodies at rest tend to stay at rest.

What I am advocating here by debunking these common misconceptions is a more realistic assessment of what technology might do for a particular institution's language curriculum. Nothing is achieved by promising the language profession a panacea for its financial and curricular woes, although many administrators would dearly like to downsize language departments using technology as a replacement. Computer technology will be a key component to most everything accomplished in the twenty-first century. The language profession needs to capitalize on its advantages and strengths by using the best teaching practices, which, in turn, should be informed by SLA theory whenever possible. By resisting the temptation to believe in the four myths outlined earlier, language teachers and administrators help open their minds to observe and contemplate instances in which technology constitutes good teaching practice. Again, teaching practice should not be totally divorced from theory (although theorists may have no interest in practice).

$<i+1>$ AND BEYOND: SLA THEORIES AND TECHNOLOGY

No general discussion of technology within the context of language teaching would be complete without a brief overview of current SLA theories. Again, the process of how a language is acquired should be kept distinct from best practices for language teaching. But it would be an unnecessary fiction to maintain that methodologies are not informed, correctly or not, by SLA theories and models.

The intent here, then, is not to explain in detail the various SLA theories and their histories; there are a number of introductory books that already meet this need (e.g., Doughty and Long 2003a; Ellis 1994, 1997; Gass and Selinker 2001; Gass 1997; Larsen-Freeman and Long 1991; VanPatten 1996). But the various SLA theories suggest differing degrees of importance concerning the role of instruction/practice and, by implication, the use of technology in the classroom. Technology, as defined earlier, is a series of electronically based platforms and tools that support many language learning activities, from the most mechanical drill-and-kill exercises to fully communicative real-time conversations (i.e., *chat*). Language professionals need to have an adequate theoretical background in order to decide when a particular tool might assist the students' linguistic development. Like the field of linguistics itself, SLA studies emanate from two distinct, but not necessarily incompatible, approaches: one that focuses attention on the psycholinguistic aspects of SLA and the other on the sociolinguistic aspects.

There is no denying that the recent interest and popularity of SLA studies owes much to Chomsky's psycholinguistic or mentalist inquiries into the nature of language, which has revolutionized the field of linguistics. Chomsky postulates that all children are innately predisposed, if not prewired, to learn language; the individual child only requires a sustained exposure (i.e., input) to one particular natural language in order to trigger the formation of an internal grammar or mental representation of linguistic competence that, in turn, governs language production or performance. According to Chomsky, this grammar-building process—known as *LAD*, the *Language Acquisition Device*, in his first theoretical formulation—is constrained by universal properties common to all languages (Chomsky 1986, 3). Through exposure to the rich linguistic input or positive evidence contained in the well-formed sentences of native speakers in the environment, the child develops all the other language-specific constructions as well. In short, language performance is a rule-governed activity generated by the child's linguistic competence or internal grammar. The occasional slips of the tongue, false starts, and memory lapses, which are part and parcel of performance, are of little importance to the linguist, who seeks to discover the underlying structures and constraints that pertain to competence, the universal core of language that makes language acquisition possible in the first place.

Krashen (1982, 1985) embraced Chomsky's ideas and adapted them to the SLA field by highlighting the role of input. But, at the same time, Krashen recognized that SLA is governed by special conditions different from first language acquisition: namely, L2 learners need input that is both challenging and assessable; they need *comprehensible input* that is within their grasp, input just slightly more complex than their current, still emerging, mental representation of the target language, or what researchers have called their interlanguage (Gass and Selinker 2001, 11). Krashen symbolized comprehensible input and its scaffolding relationship to acquisition by means of a mathematical metaphor, where i stands for *interlanguage*: $<i+1>$, input that pushes L2 learners to restructure their interlanguage without overwhelming them with data well beyond their present capabilities. Although the $<i+1>$ metaphor is somewhat dated now, given that other researchers have refined the notions of input considerably (see following discussion), Krashen's impact on the FL teaching field has been definitive. The linguistic portion of most teaching credential exams still tests Krashen's ideas almost exclusively. Likewise, most beginning FL textbooks make at least a cursory reference in their introductions to the need to present students with comprehensible input, an idea taken directly from Krashen. For this reason, I will elaborate further on Krashen's model.

Similar to Chomsky's explicit distinction between competence and performance, Krashen makes a clear distinction between the process of acquisition and that of learning. He emphasizes the subconscious nature of acquisition (i.e., competence) in contrast to the students' more conscious attempts to manipulate and learn linguistic forms (i.e., performance). Conscious learning involves monitoring and practice, but acquisition entails a change in the internal representation or competence that eventually happens with enough exposure to $<i+1>$ input. For Krashen, learned or monitored knowledge has no relationship to acquired knowledge; they are separate systems of knowledge. Other researchers (McLaughlin 1987; Gregg 1984; Swain 1985; Salaberry 1997; Ellis 2002) have argued for interrelationship between controlled processing (i.e., learning or monitoring in Krashen's terms) and the subsequent development of automatic processing, or automaticity (i.e., acquisition). In other words, after L2 learners have consciously practiced an item for a long time and no longer need to focus consciously on the structure to produce it, their responses become automatic—with the latter type of knowledge presupposing the former. With this new emphasis on more cognitive issues has also come a renewed interest in how L2 students make sense of new vocabulary, lexical chunks, and collocations in contrast to Chomsky's almost exclusive focus on formal syntactical representations as an independent and controlling module of the brain (Ellis 2002).

Krashen complements this central role assigned to comprehensible input with the sensible recognition that learning anxieties can block language acquisition for all intents and purposes. These anxieties erect an *affective filter* that reduces the students' ability to make use of comprehensible input and subsequently blocks interlanguage development. The implications he draws for the classroom should be obvious: mechanized language drills might produce some learning of forms, but the real goal of acquisition is best fostered by a communicative environment rich in comprehensible input. The communicative classroom, in addition to providing lots of comprehensible input, should also create an inviting atmosphere with an eye to lowering the students' affective filters.

Krashen's SLA model, while neither uncontroversial nor unchallenged (see Gregg 1984; Lantolf and Frawley 1988; Gass and Selinker 2001, 148–52), has had an enormous impact on classroom practice, being most closely identified with what is known as the Natural Method (Krashen and Terrell 1983). In fact, today's varied communicative approaches to language teaching all have roots in Krashen's ideas. The implementation of Krashen's theory, however, places a heavy burden on teachers to provide large amounts of comprehensible input. In other words, the theory tends to reinforce a teacher-oriented classroom, albeit one in which much language communication is happening.

Setting aside for the moment the intractable—if not unsolvable— problem of determining just what constitutes comprehensible input (i.e.,

$i+1$) for any particular L2 learner, let alone for a whole classroom of learners, the question arises as to who is to blame if the students fail to learn or progress too slowly. One interpretation would suggest that teachers have failed to provide a learning environment rich in $<i+1>$ input. But it is equally plausible that the students were unable to process crucial segments of the comprehensible input because of short-term memory problems, failure to notice certain linguistic structures, or other as yet unexplained reasons.

This is precisely what other SLA researchers have pointed out: The existence of comprehensible input in any L2 learner's environment (classroom or otherwise) does not guarantee its usefulness for SLA. Unnoticed comprehensible input is as useless as input well beyond the learner's present level of competence or interlanguage. Only when L2 learners actually notice a particular unit of input—a process that Gass and Selinker (2001, 298) have dubbed *apperception*—and can also retain that information in their short-term memories, does it become intake, or internalized input that can be used to help restructure their interlanguage grammar in more targetlike ways.

The role of consciousness and negative evidence is crucial to this revised SLA input model. L2 learners must first notice the gap between the available input and their own interlanguage (i.e., apperception) before they can develop more targetlike ways of communicating: "The first stage of input utilization is the recognition that there is something to be learned, that is, that there is a gap between what the learner already knows and what there is to know" (Gass 1997, 4). This implies that L2 learners must develop their own metalinguistic awareness—that is, a new sense that something is incorrect in their own knowledge of a second language—to stimulate a change in their interlanguage (Schmidt and Frota 1986, 306–19; Schmidt 1990).

The theoretical focus has now moved away from an examination of comprehensible input more in favor of a study of comprehended input, combined with an increased emphasis on the more social aspects of the SLA process. L2 learners discover these gaps in the course of normal communication, especially when miscommunications occur causing a breakdown in the conversational flow of information. In repairing these breakdowns through negotiations with native speakers (NS) or other non-native speakers (NNS), L2 learners tend to focus on the gaps in their linguistic knowledge. This SLA approach constitutes an interactionist model because interactionists believe that a second language is best learned—and by extension, best taught—through social interaction (Long 1981, 1991; Pica 1994; Gass 1997; Doughty 1998).

In contrast to the psycholinguistic approach, which highlights the role of positive evidence for SLA, the interactionist approach focuses on the importance of miscommunications and instances of negative evidence generated by the L2 learners' attempts to negotiate meaning with counterparts in their social (i.e., learning) environment. Miscommunications that lead to conversational negotiations either of meaning or form serve as a catalyst for change in L2 learners' linguistic knowledge, as described by Gass (1997, 87): "Through negotiation of meaning learners gain additional information about the language and focus their attention on particular parts of the language. This attention primes language for integration into a developing interlinguistic system."

Learners who are provided with information about incorrect forms are able to search for additional confirmatory or nonconfirmatory evidence. If negotiation as a form of negative evidence serves to initiate change, the factors that determine whether the initiated change results in permanent restructuring of linguistic knowledge must be identified. As with any type of learning, there needs to be reinforcement of what is being learned. In other words, acquisition appears to be gradual and, simplistically, takes time and often requires numerous doses of evidence (Gass 1997, 144–45). The interactionists are careful not to claim that negotiations of meaning cause SLA to happen but rather that these interactions are a priming device that allows learners to focus their attention on areas on which they are working (130).

A more practical instantiation of the interactionist approach is known as a *focus on form* (*FonF*; Long and Robinson 1998), a task-based methodology that calls on L2 students to solve specific tasks. As students collaborate on these tasks with other L2 learners or other NS, they focus on the source of their linguistic confusions (e.g., vocabulary, morphology, syntax), negotiate their incomplete understandings, and, consequently, analyze their own language.

In this approach, not only input, intake, and uptake but also output—forced output, to be precise—are important. Swain (1985, 2000) outlines three potential functions of output: (a) it provides the opportunity for meaningful use of one's linguistic resources, (b) it allows the learner to test hypotheses about the target language, and (c) it encourages the learner to move from semantic to syntactic processing. Swain argues that comprehension of input is a process driven by semantics; in other words, learners do not always need to parse the sentences they hear in order to arrive at the intended meaning. Production, conversely, requires the learner to utilize syntax in order to produce coherent, meaningful utterances. When a learner is pushed during output, he or she is encouraged to convey meaning in a precise and appropriate manner. This momentary "push" may be critical for language acquisition, because it promotes noticing (Swain 2000, 100): Learners may notice that they do not know how to express precisely the meaning they wish to convey at the very moment of attempting to produce it—they notice, so to speak, a "hole" in their interlanguage.

Finally, Krashen's exclusive emphasis on input led the FL profession to eschew any type of explicit linguistic explanations; for example, the Natural Method prefers to rely only on implicit forms of instruction. The FonF studies, along with other lines of inquiry, have reaffirmed the role that explicit instruction might play in the SLA process (MacWhinney 1997; Ellis 2002). This marks a significant change in attitude concerning the computer, a tool that can be used particularly well in support of explicit language instruction.

SLA THEORY, INTERACTIONS, AND THE COMPUTER

Most computer programs minimally do something in response to mouse clicks, data entry, or other keyboard actions: they beep, show a picture file, move to another screen, play digital sounds, or the like. These minimal computer reactions often constitute the sole basis for commercially labeling the program as interactive. How does this sense of the word fare against the more social and interactionist definition described earlier? For the interactionists, L2 learners are motivated to learn new structures by being incited by other speakers to use the target language. In fact, for many language professionals technology might represent the antithesis of what learning a second language should be all about: talking to and interacting with real *people* in the target language.

Nevertheless, the computer's obvious failings as a person (including Kubrick's infamous computer HAL from *2001*) are relatively unimportant in the face of how people work with computers. As mentioned earlier,

Reeves and Nass (1996, 5) have shown that people have a strong tendency to interact with computer machines in a fundamentally social manner, just like interactions in real life. These social scientists argue for the existence of a media equation where media can equal real-life experiences. For example, if a computer program addresses users in a polite fashion, then the users will respond politely as well, even though they know in purely intellectual terms that a machine has no feelings. According to Reeves and Nass, programs that capitalize on the media equation usually solicit more favorable reactions from computer users than programs that ignore the media equation. In other words, L2 learners conceive of the computer as their own personal helper rather than the mindless, heartless tool that it really is. This inherent tendency to anthropomorphize our world—from our cars to our pets—persists and gives technology its potential to assist the SLA process. People think computers are trying to help them and respond, as in any human relationship, by making a best-faith effort to cooperate.

Good interface design builds on this fiction. It is not necessary for computers to be human but only to simulate certain human qualities. Above all, people count on computers to follow basic Gricean principles (Pinker 1994 [1995], 228): namely, that the information supplied is relevant, truthful, informative, clear, unambiguous, brief, and orderly. This is especially true if programs can be designed to intervene or provide feedback that is well suited or relevant to the particular user's needs. Fogg (2003, 38) calls this the principle of tailoring: "Information provided by computing technology will be more persuasive if it is tailored to the individual's needs, interests, personality, usage context, or other factors relevant to the individual." Fogg (69–70) also formulates two other principles of virtual rehearsals and rewards, which states that positive reinforcement or rewards received from computer programs can cause human beings to rehearse behavior with a carryover in attitudes and conduct to the real world. In a word, people expect good input from the computer and therein lies its power to help students learn.

QUO VADIS?

We have come full circle from the outset of the chapter. Input, especially comprehended input, is one of the basic cornerstones of current SLA theories:

Without input, SLA can't occur; it is a necessary condition but not the only one—it's not a sufficient condition. Technology, then, if cleverly designed and properly implemented into the curriculum, has a vital role to play in augmenting the opportunities for L2 learners to receive target-language input. Again, the learners' contact with the target language is a critical factor for the SLA process, which normally takes five to seven years under classroom conditions, as most FL professionals working in the trenches already know.

An increasingly multicultural world in global and local contexts will put intense pressure on our profession to find the most efficient and readily accessible ways to learn another language. To that end, using technology is a challenge that language professionals must squarely face and to which they must endeavor to find pedagogically principled responses. Theory must be combined with practice, which will not happen without our colleagues' willingness to experiment with the newest modes of teaching with technology. While FL teachers and students alike need to acquire a basic degree of functional computer literacy, they must also learn to exercise a critical literacy as consumers of technology and, eventually, a rhetorical literacy as future producers of technology (see Selber 2004 and further discussion in chapter 6). In order words, Dreamweaver, chat applications, blogs, wikis, JavaScript, or any other tricks of the trade are just a beginning that opens the doors to more student-directed activities and the L2 student's journey toward self-definition and identity as a multilingual/multicultural speaker, quite apart from whatever identity may be attributed to the ubiquitous but anonymous native speaker.[7]

In the following three chapters, I look closely at three platforms—the web, CD-ROM/DVD programs, and CMC—always with an eye to establishing what a basic, functional computer literacy should be, and then looking forward in the true humanistic spirit to both a critical and rhetorical literacy as well. In chapters 5 and 6 I put all the tools together to suggest how the new technologically assisted curriculum will work in both a distance learning and a classroom context and what research issues remain to be examined.

DISCUSSION QUESTIONS AND ACTIVITIES

1.   What are researchers in SLA referring to when they speak of L2 competence versus L2 performance and L2 acquisition versus L2

learning? Can performance be separated from competence? Into which category would L2 pragmatics fall (i.e., the knowledge about the appropriate situational context for words, utterances, and meanings)?

2.   Imagine that you have to convince your colleagues, who are mostly interested in literature, to make an investment in using technology for the FL curriculum. List five reasons why it is also in their interests to support your plan. Consider scientific as well as social reasons that provide an incentive for your department's investment in technology.

3.   What would you say to your colleagues in order to ease their worries that investing in technology will not eliminate language-teaching jobs?

4.   Discuss whether it is a problem or an advantage for language teachers that this generation of incoming students will most likely know more about using certain technological tools than they do.

5.   Conduct a web search for the following theme: language teaching with technology. Share your results with a colleague or classmate.

6.   Debate which aspects of Krashen's theories about SLA are well grounded and which are not supported given recent advances in the SLA field.

NOTES

1. SLA theorists often make a distinction between foreign language acquisition, where instruction occurs in a place in which the target language is not spoken, and second language acquisition, where instruction occurs in a target-language speaking country. Throughout this book I use the term "second language acquisition (SLA)" to refer to both circumstances indiscriminately.
2. These figures are taken from the report listed at www.translate-to-success.com/online-language-web-site-content.html.
3. Cummins (personal communication) estimates that five to seven years are needed to reach academic proficiency on the English CALP exam, a figure quite consonant with the FSI's experience in teaching second languages.

4. *Interactive* is a loaded term nowadays. It has come to mean any program that includes user-responsiveness, but, in fact, true interactivity supports reciprocal actions (Laurillard 2002, 107). Only CMC (see chapter 4) can truly be said to provide that level of interactivity.
5. See the special issue of the *CALICO Journal* 17, no. 2 (2000).
6. Our knowledge of SLA still remains quite modest, as Richard Schmidt has characterized in a recent talk at the University of California, Davis, April 2005, in terms of "Fifty (probably) true and (possibly) useful findings from SLA."
7. Kramsch (2000) has written extensively arguing against the construct of NS, especially as the desired endpoint for the L2 learner.

Chapter 2

Web Pages in Service of L2 Learning

THE WEB IN NON-ENGLISH LANGUAGES?

The growth of the World Wide Web (WWW, or more simply, the web) in recent years has been nothing short of staggering: from 2002 to 2005 the number of Internet users has increased by 183 percent (Internet World Stats, 2006). More important for American educational circles, a recent survey by the Pew Foundation reports that nine out of ten teenage school children, ages twelve through seventeen, have online access (Lenhart, Madden, and Hitlin 2005, 2). These children predominantly use the Internet to process e-mails (89%), browse for information about movies or public figures (84%), play games (81%), read the daily news (76%), send instant messages (75%), shop for colleges (57%), or buy merchandise online (43%). If FL instructors stop for a moment to contemplate the fact that these same children will soon populate their classes in the higher education system, the rationale and motivation to incorporate technology into the language curriculum becomes quite clear: It is a medium that our students understand, pay attention to, and like to use.[1] The same cannot be said about teachers; many language teachers resist investing in technology for the curriculum for a variety of reasons, including personal teaching philosophies, time-honored beliefs, and additional time burdens (Arnold and Ducate 2006).

Despite its pervasiveness, some language professionals might still question the suitability of the web for the FL curriculum because English appears to be the de facto official language of the Internet. In the American context, again, predictions abound that the entire world will end up just using English to communicate not only on the web but also in all business and diplomatic contexts.

Setting aside for the moment the obvious political and cultural reasons that argue against such an eventuality (but see the discussion in the follow-

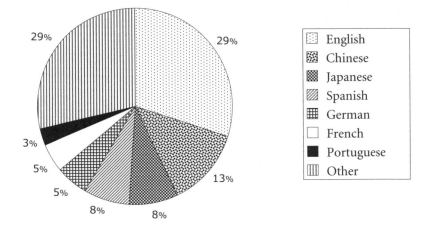

Figure 2.1   Internet Users by Language

ing section), the facts about world language usage on the Internet appear to contradict the idea that English will eliminate the other languages on the web. Internet World Stats (2006) reports that 29.7 percent of the approximately 1 billion Internet users access the web in English—and this includes NNS or speakers of so-called *world English*.[2] Although English speakers clearly constitute the largest group of Internet users (see figure 2.1), a majority of the world's Internet users prefer to surf the web in their native language, with the top users accessing in Chinese (13.3%), Japanese (7.9%), Spanish (7.5%), and German (5.4%); (Internet World Stats, 2006). Furthermore, the non-English usage for these four languages is increasing at a faster rate than for English, with Chinese leading the way (Grefenstette 2000; Warschauer and De Florio-Hansen 2003).

Fortunately, the advent of Unicode font standards has made displaying web pages and typing in languages other than English relatively easy, as Godwin-Jones has so clearly explained for the FL profession (Godwin-Jones 2002). Both Macs and PCs allow the user to change the method of keyboard input on the fly, making switching from English to Arabic or any other languages a trivial matter, as long as the writing program or browser supports Unicode.

There are far more important cultural reasons that will establish the web as a place of multilingual and multicultural expression. Sociolinguistic research informs us that language always functions as an identity marker in addition to fulfilling its role as a tool of communications and information transfer. Accordingly, people will always prefer to surf the web in their native language, whether they are consuming or selling information or, more important, projecting a public self-image (for an illustration of how a Hawaiian community defines the terms of its own self-reference, see Warschauer and De Florio-Hansen 2003). In other words, the web gives all people a relatively uncontrolled channel to project their own voice and promote their own particular view of reality.

This helps to explain why non-English web pages continue to grow despite the English language's dominant role in the world as a scientific and business lingua franca. Kramsch (1993) has long made it clear to our profession that learning another language presents an opportunity for a critical interrogation of the very notion of culture (also see Lange, Klee, Paige, and Yershova 2000). The web directly provides primary source materials in pursuit of this intellectual inquiry, especially through searches commonly known as *webquests* (Godwin-Jones 2004; Chen 2006), an inquiry-oriented activity based on web sources. Dodge (2002) provides language teachers with a breakdown of the type of webquest tasks students might undertake: retellings, compilations, mystery hunts, journalistic reports, design projects, creative products, consensus building, persuasive discourses, self-knowledge searches, analyses, judgment tasks, and scientific inquiries.

This is not to say that the Internet is a culturally neutral tool or that viewing multimedia materials on the web reduces the need to interpret what we see and read, as Kramsch and Anderson (1999) have already pointed out in their study of students using online Quechua language pages. In other words, the use of the web, far from diminishing the importance of the classroom experience and the role of the teacher, imbues classroom discussion with even more value, if the L2 teacher knows how to take advantage of the medium (see the following discussion for further suggestions). Each L2 student needs to become a researcher on the web, an interpreter of culture, a careful note taker of cross-cultural differences with any mediating effects occasioned by the medium itself (Dubreil 2006, 252–56).

Although the web can be directly harnessed for oral tasks and activities, one of its greatest strengths lies in providing opportunities to reflect on literacy and interpretation. This is why I argued in chapter 1 that literature professors have an equal stake in promoting the use and best practices of a technologically assisted FL curriculum. The goals of a technologically assisted language curriculum feed the same interests of the upper-division program in humanities.

In the following sections, I survey some of the basic technical constructs of the web, introduce additional tools and extensions that enrich the Internet's use, and finally, discuss a number of recent pedagogical approaches to web pages that are consonant with the established SLA theories outlined in chapter 1.

INTERNET BASICS

To get started in the use of the web in service to the L2 curriculum, it is helpful to know where the Internet came from and what it was originally designed to do. Regardless of whether you intend to produce your own web pages, a few basic notions about the HTML programming language that makes a web page so attractive when viewed by a browser, file management, multimedia tools, and hosting are necessary before launching into more advanced web page tricks or even designing a pedagogically sound web lesson.[3]

Roots of the Internet

In chapter 3 of *The Virtual Community* (2000), Rheingold chronicles the development of the web from its humble beginnings as ARPANET, a project funded in the 1960s and 1970s by the U.S. Department of Defense's Advanced Research Projects Agency (DARPA). This project allowed a small group of unorthodox and visionary computer programmers and electronic engineers to redesign the way computers operated so that people could engage in interactive computing. While two more decades of research and development passed before their ideas became a reality, this basic experiment laid the foundation for the computer network known today as the World Wide Web. In 1969, there were only a thousand ARPANET users, in contrast to the billion plus web surfers online in 2006.

In 1983, ARPANET split into ARPANET for research and MILNET for military operational use. Both systems provided a wide-area backbone network with high-speed access to communicate among their own backbone nodes in a completely distributed fashion. This structure provided the basis for an explosive growth of nodes and networks that expanded the original capacity and concept of ARPANET. In 1986, the National Science Foundation (NSF) initiated a networked dubbed NSFNET that created a hub of interconnected supercomputer centers around the United States, which has evolved into the Internet's main backbone. ARPANET was decommissioned in 1990, leaving the NSF's interconnected supercomputing centers as the sole public infrastructure for online communications or, more simply, the Internet. This historical background explains why the often-employed metaphor of the electronic highway, made up of interconnecting roads of varying sizes and traffic, is so apt in describing the Internet. Anyone with a connection to some road that leads into the system can use the Internet.

The spirit and legacy of the original inventors of ARPANET and NSFNET lives on too. From the security side of things, the decentralized packet-switching technology that made the Internet function correctly also renders controlling or disabling this communication system almost impossible. The original inventors were worried about the effects of a massive nuclear attack. The digitized packet-switching technology permitted a network of routers to move information (i.e., text, sound, graphics, programs, and video) around the network, even when certain nodes had ceased to function. This feature democratized the web so that no single individual could control it and dictate policy to anyone else. Even today anyone can run a web server and post web pages for the entire world to see.

The other principal intent of the Internet's creators was to empower humans to think better wherever they found themselves: on the road, at work, or at home. In other words, anytime/anywhere computing: a way of giving power to users. Accordingly, user autonomy became the norm, a key feature of today's Internet. Recast in more educational terms, the very nature of the Internet is designed to encourage student-centered learning rather than teacher-centered learning, a major focus of task-based or content-based instruction. Lai and Zhao (2005, 405) point out that the very hypertextual nature of the Web affords L2 learners greater control over their own learning processes—that is, more flexible learning paths (hopefully, in more meaningful ways). In addition, this feature may lower students' affective filter, in Krashen's sense of the term.

Getting Started

Launching onto the web for the first time is relatively easy. First, you need a wired or wireless Internet connection via modem (which uses the phone lines to reach a computer node), an Internet service provider (ISP), or a T1 connection that links directly to a main network node. Second, you need a *browser* program such as Internet Explorer, Netscape, FireFox, Mozilla, or Safari in order to read web pages written in compliance with an international standard for *hypertext transfer protocol* (*HTTP*) using a *hypertext markup language,* or *HTML* code. Finally, you need a web page address, or a *uniform resource locator* (*URL*). Online manuals for getting started on the web abound and can be found via Internet search using search words such as "guide to the Internet" (e.g., www.learnthenet.com). Blyth (1999) offers a comprehensible and friendly guide to the web from a FL perspective, as does Fidelman (1995–96). These two publications continue to be useful to the beginner despite their relatively early publication dates, but a few basic concepts such as URLs and HTML coding deserve some additional attention.

URLs, HTML, File Management, and Language Lab

Composing web pages yourself is more complicated than viewing them. In this section and the following section on advanced tools, I provide more details on what goes into making a publicly available web page than what some beginners might want to tackle on the first go-around. Very often novice web composers simply use personal blogs (see chapter 4) to produce web pages because little technical knowledge is needed. Other beginners can count on expert help from internet technology (IT) or language lab personnel. The reader should feel free to skip over those details that seem too burdensome for the moment.

Table 2.1   URL Syntax

Protocol	Host Name	Domain	Directory Path	Filename
http://	LooneyTunes.ucdavis	.edu/	~Jones/	filename.html/
http://	www.learnthenet	.com/	english/	index.html/
http://	www.axis	.org/	usarios/	farocena
http://	www.asp	.net/	whitepaper/	whyaspnet.aspx?tabindex=0/
http://	www4.army	.mil/	outreach/	index2.html/
http://	national.gallery	.ca/		
		.gov/		

Web pages from anywhere in the world can be viewed by means of a web browser if the user enters the correct URL. Web pages follow a protocol or scheme for delivering and retrieving multimedia information known as HTTP. Web pages are primarily written or coded in HTML, a standardized programming language for the web, although more interactive enhancements can be added with JavaScript and CGI scripts. URLs follow a particular syntax, as illustrated in table 2.1.

The first item of a URL entry begins by declaring HTTP as the protocol so the browser can recognize and read it. The second item refers to the server or host name (e.g., "LooneyTunes") or a generic default such as "www" or "www4" followed by more specific location information (e.g., the name of a university, a business, an organization, a branch of government). The domain indicates the type of entity that manages the web page: an educational institution (.edu), a for-profit business (.com), a nonprofit organization (.org), a special network of people (.net), or the military network (.mil); sometimes the URL gives further information such as country of origin (e.g., .ca, .mex, .es, .fr, .de).

The URL address examined up to this point constitutes the bare minimum for a working URL, but it might also contain additional information relating to the file's pathway (e.g., ~Jones, english, whitepaper, outreach, usarios), often followed by the exact file name for a particular web page (e.g., filename.html, index.html, whyaspnet.aspx?tabindex=0). Most file names carry the extension .html or .htm to confirm that the page is coded in a standard fashion. The tilde (~) identifies the pathway that belongs to a specific individual rather than a group. A URL address is always case sensitive: for example, *filename* is not the same entry as *Filename*.

HTTP is not the only protocol that is used on the Internet. A list of other common protocols follows:

- **ftp:** indicates a resource to be retrieved using *FTP* (*file transfer protocol*), usually a file located on a so-called FTP server, a file on a particular computer; an FTP file cannot be read by a web browser—a separate FTP program is needed to move it somewhere (the desktop or to a server)
- **gopher:** signals a distributed document search of Gopher servers, a system used early on, especially by libraries, but this system has been largely supplanted by the web
- **mailto:** initiates a mail command to an electronic mail address
- **news:** refers to a newsgroup or an article in Usenet news
- *telnet:* starts an interactive session via the telnet protocol

The FTP protocol is particularly important for L2 teachers because they can use these addresses to send and receive files back and forth from the desktop to a public web server—especially large multimedia files with graphics, audio, and video. Moving files to and from a server requires a different program from that of a browser: an FTP program such as Fetch, Fugu, Ipwitch, Core, WS_FTP, just to name a few options, most of which can be downloaded for free from the web.

The process of composing a web page has become relatively easy with the advent of programs such as Macromedia's Dreamweaver, Microsoft's Front-Page, Adobe's PageMill, Mozilla's Composer, and AOLPress. Even Word allows an author to save a document in HTML source code. Despite the ease of using one of these *what-you-see-is-what-you-get* (*WYSIWYG*) web editors, L2 teachers should have a minimum understanding of the syntax that makes HTML source code turn into attractive web pages when viewed with a browser application.

HTML code consists of a series of tags that tell the browser what to do with the materials nested inside them. Every tag comes in pairs: the beginning of the tag and the end of the tag. The first and most necessary pair of tags for any source code simply states that what follows is written in HTML: for example,

<HTML> . . . </HTML>. Everything in the middle of this pair of tags should be interpreted according to the HTTP protocol. Consider the following sample of HTML source code written to produce a very simple web page, as adapted from Arocena's (2006, chap. 4) HTML tutorials written in Spanish.[4]

```
<HTML>
<HEAD>
<TITLE> My Web Page – lesson 4 </TITLE>
</HEAD>
<BODY>
<CENTER>
<H1> My Web Page </H1>
</CENTER>
<HR>
This is my Web page. It's rather simple, but I hope you like it.
<P> <A HREF="hobbies.html"> <IMG SRC="man.gif"> </A> My
hobbies
<P> <A HREF="favorites.html"> <IMG SRC="house.gif"> </A> My
favorite pages
<CENTER>
<H3> The ideal place for a vacation </H3>
<IMG SRC="island.gif" ALT="island">
</CENTER>
</BODY>
</HTML>
```

This source code has a separate section enclosed by <HEAD> . . . </HEAD> and, later, another section called <BODY> . . . </BODY>. The title of the web page (which appears in the title bar of the browser) is nested within the HEAD tags; the main information of the web page is inserted between the BODY tags. The actual text of the web page can be formatted for size by different headers (<H1> or <H3>), for alignment (<CENTER>), and for spacing (<P>). Remember that all text and/or multimedia files must be nested between a beginning tag and an ending tag.

The ANCHOR tag (<A>) found in the code is used to create hyperlinks: for example, <A HREF="hobbies.html"> <IMG SRC="man.gif"> </A>. In this case, the ANCHOR tag (<A>) allows the web user to click on a picture or image source (IMG SRC = man.gif) and link it to a different web page named hobbies.html. The same sort of hyper-referencing (<A HREF = . . . >) or hyperlinking could also be anchored to a single word or series of words: for example, <A HREF="hobbies.html"> Click on this sentence to see a list of my hobbies </A>. When viewed with a browser, then, this source code would display the words "Click on this sentence to see a list of my hobbies" in a special color (usually blue to indicate a hyperlink), and clicking on it would take you to the other web page named hobbies.html. In other words, the ANCHOR tags specify both a link (i.e., reference) and an anchor point.

Source code can be copied from existing web pages (while running a browser application, select SOURCE under the VIEW menu, or right-click and select PROPERTIES and then SOURCE), pasted into a HTML editor, modified, saved as an HTML document, and subsequently viewed locally as a web page by a browser program. If the same HTML file is transferred via an FTP program to a server on the web, it becomes public and anyone with the corresponding URL can view the same page. But a word of caution is in order. The simple source code given earlier points to three graphics files in gif format—man.gif, house.gif, island.gif—and two additional text files (hobbies.html, favorites.html). These five files must all be transferred to and reside on the same server and in the same area or folder. If that is not the case, the web page will break (i.e., it will not display the correct links).

Creating functional and striking web pages, then, is much like putting together an intricate salad: all of the ingredients must be present, moved around or tossed, and served according to protocol if Internet users are going to consume it. Figure 2.2 is meant to capture the creation process for a web page, including the notion of proper file management.

For the novice web creator, managing the different pieces of multimedia can be challenging, even frustrating, despite the transparency of the process as outlined in figure 2.2. Likewise, producing audio clips, video clips, and animated files that make web pages so interesting and interactive requires additional knowledge of other multimedia tools. Using multimedia files often requires an additional download and installation of a plug-in or web extension program in order to make everything execute properly (e.g., Flash, QuickTime, Shockwave, Java).

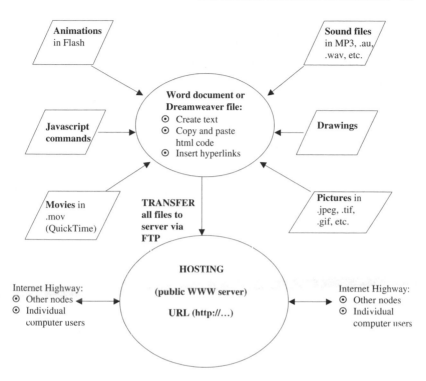

Figure 2.2 Creation of a Published Web Page

Ideally, all L2 teachers using technology should be supported and trained by the staff in a language lab or university computer lab. The language lab constitutes an intimate part of an institution's infrastructure, much like the library. The International Association for Language Learning Technology, or IALLT (www.iallt.org/), has published a detailed description of the professional responsibilities and services that language lab personnel should provide. Even an advanced web page user or producer will need assistance from time to time; this is just the nature of a medium that is constantly changing (remember myth 3 from chapter 1: *Technology will not change.*).

Similarly, institutions should provide their teachers with space where web pages can be *hosted* or placed on a public web server. Space becomes crucial, especially if large amounts of digitized audio and/or video are included in the web curriculum. Hosting should be considered part of the general infrastructure of any educational enterprise. Nevertheless some schools or school districts cannot afford to maintain a server for their instructors. In that case, individuals can purchase hosting privileges for relatively modest prices by shopping around on the Internet.

FL Dictionaries, Links, and Search Engines

Many lists of favorite FL links already exist on the web as a result of previous efforts by individuals and university language labs.[5] When FL teachers were just beginning to exploit the web in service of the FL curriculum, much energy went into developing long lists of URLs without much thought as to how they might used. In addition to not providing a pedagogical framework for using the web, these efforts ran into problems from *link rot,* or inactive, moved, or defunct links, a phenomenon that occurs with great frequency on the web, as it is a constantly changing network.

As with any new print materials included in the FL curriculum, teachers should ask themselves what they will want students to do with Internet resources. But teachers should realize that link rot can affect even pedagogically well-designed web materials and render them useless when a key hyperlink is broken. To get around this problem, many L2 teachers ask their students to carry out their own searches for FL materials, usually guided by a list of key words that the instructors provide. Obviously, the teacher should test those key words beforehand to make sure that they produce a variety of acceptable results for the task at hand.

Today's students are quite familiar with performing web searches via a search engine such as Google, Yahoo!Search, or MSN Search. By using these tools or similar ones, students can retrieve primary source information in the target language. Likewise, online FL dictionaries and digital newspapers are available for most of the world's languages. The FLTEACH listserv offers a particularly comprehensive list of materials resources, as well as many other professional development uses (LeLoup and Ponterio 2004).[6]

ENHANCING WEB INTERACTIVITY: ADVANCED TOOLS

Without a pedagogy wrapped around them, reading web pages presents students with a relatively static activity; fortunately, certain advanced web programming tricks can increase a web page's level of (inter)activity.

On the one hand, these more sophisticated techniques are not for the beginner. On the other, every FL instructor should develop a help network or have access to a cyber-guru who is cognizant of what these advanced techniques can provide L2 students. By default, the most obvious cyber-guru for the L2 teacher should be the staff at the language lab or the university computer center. But teachers should not discount the knowledge of other colleagues who have acquired web knowledge through experience. Two excellent sources of advanced tips are the "On the Net" and "Emerging Technologies" columns written for the online journal *Language, Learning, and Technology* (http://llt.msu.edu). Many web-page enhancements are realized by creating Java applets, adding CGI scripts, inserting JavaScript into the standard HTML source code, and/or writing pages in dynamic HTML or DHTML coding. I will treat each of these topics separately in the following sections, with appreciation to Godwin-Jones's (1998) expert explanations.

I have already mentioned the use of miniprograms called plug-ins that allow for animation extensions derived from programs produced by Flash and Shockwave. In a similar fashion, Java, a full-fledged programming language from Sun, Inc., can be used to create miniprograms that can be fully integrated with web pages to perform sophisticated functions such as chat programs with sound, interactive quizzes, and questionnaires, just to name a few applications.

JavaScript refers to a scripting language that shares a syntactic structure similar to Java but only operates within a web browser. Clearly, JavaScript lacks the power and independence that Java offers, but it is much easier to learn and to use. The JavaScript commands can be embedded directly into the regular HTML source code in order to perform functions such as quiz self-corrections and responses to mouse clicks or cursor movements. Godwin-Jones (1998) also highlights JavaScript's ability to work with form elements on a web page such as radio buttons, check boxes, or text fields without having to send the data to a web server. All the interaction is carried out locally within the user's web browser, and it therefore executes its program very fast. JavaScript is not a compiled program; it can be inserted into other HTML code with any text or web editor. As with any web page source code, JavaScript can also be copied and pasted into other web pages. WYSIWYG page editors now facilitate adding JavaScript to your web page by means of pull-down menus that automatically add the necessary code.

An older (and, perhaps, less secure) method of extracting data from a web form involves writing *CGI script* (*Common Gateway Interface*) in *PERL*, a programming language, and then placing it on a web server. When the web forms are submitted, the CGI script takes the data from the form, analyzes it, stores it in a database, and then sends feedback to the user in the form of another web page or e-mail message. Only an experienced cyber-guru with network training or a lab technician would be capable of setting up this type of CGI script, but once installed only the address for the CGI scripts is needed to use the FORM command provided by a WYSIWYG editor like Dreamweaver or FrontPage.

Finally, dynamic HTML, or DHTML, can be added to web pages to allow certain features of the page to be changed according to user choices entered in on the fly. Godwin-Jones (1998, 10) extols the benefits of DHTML: "With DHTML the goal is to make virtually everything on the Web page able to be changed in reaction to user actions. This includes the possibility of knowing where on the page a user has clicked. By making everything on a Web page both *hot* and changeable, a dynamic environment is being created with functionality similar to what is possible with traditional multimedia authoring systems. Typeface, color, size, visibility, position, and other attributes can all be manipulated on the fly or in response to users' actions."

Just like JavaScript, the interactivity that DHTML offers the user is defined and operationalized locally; no communication with another web server is required, as in the case of CGI scripts.

TOWARD A PEDAGOGY FOR WEB-BASED LANGUAGE LEARNING

The technical information imparted in the previous sections is a prerequisite for both consumers and producers of FL web pages but is not sufficient for the L2 teacher wishing to implement technology in service of an L2 curriculum. Without a clear pedagogy for web-based language learning, the best applications of technology will be for naught (remember myth 2, *Technology [by itself] constitutes a methodology*) and abandons the student to nothing more than a series of navigable resources (URLs) accompanied by fill-in-the-blank exercises. Having already examined in previous sections some of the web's distinct advantages—especially those of information access in foreign languages and the possibilities for learner control—I now reflect on how teachers must integrate these materials into the FL curriculum to gain the maximum benefits; again, teachers remain the most crucial link in creating a successful web-based language curriculum. Unfortunately teachers tend to focus on the web exclusively to solve the eternal problem of how to teach grammar.

The problem can be illustrated by analyzing a typical title from a paper given at a recent national conference on language teaching: "Using Authentic Web-based Materials to Teach Grammar in Context." At first blush, this presentation sounds reasonable, maybe even exemplary in its goals—it is certainly not unique but rather representative of what many teachers wish to accomplish with their own web pages: to teach grammar in context. (Isn't that a good thing?) Its authors contend that the grammar activities presented therein can be adapted to all foreign languages with only a few minor adjustments. Web materials of this ilk are usually produced following a predictable algorithm: (a) identify a web reading or web video clip in the target language that contains a particular linguistic structure to be practiced (e.g., the Spanish subjunctive, the French *passé simple*, the German passive voice); (b) link photos and graphics from the web; (c) add sound files recorded by native speakers; and (d) ask the students to fill in the blanks with the correct form of the verb. This type of web page reflects a grammar-driven pedagogy that assumes that technology can best help L2 students practice grammar online in order to free up more time for conversation in class (for a critique of the grammar-driven uses of technology, see Garrett 1988; for additional examples of grammar-driven pages, see LeLoup and Ponterio 2003). This formula for producing web pages assumes that everything is better if accompanied by multimedia (i.e., myth 2).

Every FL teacher has written exercises like this at one time or another, whether in paper or web form, but the disconnect with the true goals of FL education should be self-evident—students need practice in engaging in real-life interactions, not just discrete grammar exercises (for a more in-depth critique, see Brandl 2002). While contextualized exercises of this type may be superior to the de-contextualized ones used by the translation method, this approach still falls short of taking proper advantage of the web's access to authentic materials and the possibilities for both student autonomy and collaboration. Exercises like these present students with a more elegant type of drill-and-kill computer exercise but still not very different in function from the dominant form of exercises common in the early stages of the CALL field (Garrett 1986, 1988).

Arguably, there is nothing intrinsically wrong with incorporating grammar exercises into the curriculum, even the drill-and-kill type, especially in the beginning stages of learning a new language where new morphology and syntactic structures present so many challenges to the L2 learner. But drill-and-kill should not constitute the driving concept behind a web-based L2 curriculum. Best practices would dictate that teachers should try to adapt their web lessons into a framework such as FonF (see chapter 1) that puts the negotiation of meaning at the center of its implementation.

To avoid the curricular pitfall described earlier, I turn now to some central educational notions and ask, "What are FL teachers trying to achieve?" Laurillard (2002, 23) of the British Open University identifies the general goals of university teaching: "Teaching is essentially a rhetorical activity, seeking to persuade students to change the way they experience the world through an understanding of the insights of others. It has to create the environment that enables students to embrace the twin poles of experiential and formal knowledge." If applied to language teaching, Laurillard's goals highlight two important concepts only briefly touched on earlier: (a) language learning (or teaching) is a mediated or negotiated process, an endeavor best carried out within an interactionist framework (see chapter 1); and (b) learning an L2 involves the development of a new sense of identity that blends insights from both L1 and L2. The latter refers to the desire for L2 students to develop a sense of the other without losing their own sense of self—what Kramsch, A'Ness, and Lam (2000) have dubbed the tension between authenticity (from the web) and authorship (from the L2 learner).

Formal knowledge, such as grammar and the like, remains important but needs to be taught in a manner that Laurillard (2002, 13–16) describes as situated knowledge, knowledge that deals with real-world activities. In other words, the curriculum should not treat the body of conceptual knowledge to be learned as separate from the situation in which it is to be used. Accordingly, this educational philosophy nudges the FL teacher to rethink how to incorporate authentic materials along with the activities that students are asked to perform with them in order to bring the students' potential contributions into the learning equation.

All learning environments afford certain benefits as well as incur disadvantages for learning—the web-based environment being no exception (for a less optimistic view of using the web, see Vogel 2001). The web's multimedia medium allows teachers to focus in particular on authentic texts in wondrous ways. Teachers can fashion reading assignments supported by multimedia glosses (sound, video, text) that are simply unavailable in print form (Chun and Plass 1997).[7] A reading task delivered in a web format can also provide attractive cultural sidebars and background information that seek to focus the students' attention and stimulate them to read and explore the L2 culture even more (Osuna and Meskill 1998). Textbooks attempt to do the same with fancy color layouts and design, but the web environment offers an organic, ever-changing medium with palpable and proven ways of grabbing students' attention.

For instance, web pages can include sound files that harness a sensorial channel lacking in books. Sound files increase the prospects of building lasting mental images for words and phrases in a phonological, semantic, and even aesthetic context. While reading the web version of a Lorca poem, to cite one example of many, the L2 student can simultaneously hear the poetry recited aloud so that the words come alive. Clearly, these types of affordances affect the poem's reception. The same could be said of web texts of a more prosaic nature: interviews, commercials, recipes, and business slogans. Likewise, a similar supporting role can be invented for visual imagery, another one of the web's strong points.

But none of these web affordances relieve the teacher from preparing a pathway for students to engage web reading that is accompanied by the appropriate battery of prereading strategies such as an advance organizer, extensive and intensive reading activities, cognate study, and a follow-up application (Phillips 1984). Chun (2006, 81) reports that background knowledge of an authentic reading accounts for nearly 28 percent of the variance in student comprehension rates, especially for intermediate readers. Salaberry (2001, 51) claims, "The success of a technology-driven activity will likely depend as much or more, on the successful accomplishment of pre- and post-activities than on the technology activity itself." Accordingly, only by means of a well-constructed lesson can L2 students progress from being passive consumers of authentic source materials (on the web or in print) to active authors/owners of the material in the sense discussed by Kramsch, A'Ness, and Lam (2000). In addition, Laurillard (2002, 112) warns that the web's nonlinear nature demands that teachers map out a learning pathway so that students don't become lost in constructing their own narrative line.

Some techniques for helping students construct meaning in a web environment undoubtedly require more interactive or communicative tools that go beyond simple reading strategies performed in isolation. To accomplish this online, teachers must resort to a dialogic or conversational framework (see Laurillard 2002). In chapter 4 I discuss using the Internet to communicate (i.e., CMC) and describe its potential for transforming the student's online experience.

For the moment let us return to the topic of web pages and to every FL teacher's nagging worry, the same worry lurking beneath the cited conference title: how to teach the L2 grammar—pronunciation, vocabulary, and syntax. Can technology really help us carry out this task in a way that improves on sterile de-contextualized exercises and supersedes even the more contextualized web-mediated fill-in-the-blank exercises? Yes, it's possible, but another general educational philosophy must be brought to bear on the problem: *Content-Based Instruction (CBI*; see Stryker and Leaver 1997). It's a matter of linking and engaging the students' (pre)conceptions with their contact with new experiences and getting them to put their newly acquired knowledge into action: The teacher's job is to mediate between the poles of experiential and formal knowledge (Laurillard 2002, 23).

CONTENT-BASED INSTRUCTION (CBI) AND THE TEACHING OF GRAMMAR

CBI , in its essence, recommends a top-down constructivist approach based on Vygotsky's (1962) ideas whereby teachers facilitate their students' involvement in real-world task analysis, problem generation, and assessment grounded in real-world activities (Laurillard 2002, 67).[8] Above all, a CBI curriculum strives for language activities that are student-centered rather than teacher-centered (for examples of well-designed web tasks, see Brandl 2002; Warschauer 1995; and Lomicka and Cooke-Plagwitz 2004) and offers an alternative to the piecemeal, bottom-up approaches common to most grammar-driven curricula (Stryker and Leaver 1997, 3). The target language largely serves as the vehicle through which subject matter content is learned rather than as the immediate object of study (Brinton, Snow, and Wesche 1989, 5; Crandall and Tucker 1990, 187). Genesee (1994, 3) further suggests that content in a CBI curriculum need not be strictly academic (i.e., only dealing with traditional subjects such as math, history, science, geography, and the arts); it can include any topic, theme, or nonlanguage issue of interest or importance to the L2 learner. Accordingly CBI promotes negotiation of meaning, which is known to enhance language acquisition (Lightbrown and Spada 1993), in part because the tasks are intrinsically interesting, self-motivating, and cognitively engaging (Byrnes 2000; Brown 2001). Historically the CBI approach formed the cornerstone methodology for the Canadian immersion programs of the 1960s (Stryker and Leaver 1997, 15).

In a CBI approach, developing web-based grammar tutorials is not so much about finding a web text with lots of target-language subjunctive, passive voice, past tenses, or any other specific linguistic structure. In practical terms, this means that a CBI approach might present learners with authentic materials containing grammatical structures not seen before or well beyond their present capacity, as opposed to using graded language texts. Stryker and Leaver (1997) offer the following suggestions for dealing with the linguistic difficulties that authentic materials so favored by the CBI approach might engender:

> CBI teachers can find themselves routinely working with materials that are, in the traditional view, far beyond the current linguistic expertise of their students. In such a case, the important issue is not so much what those texts are but what the teacher does with them. If the teacher carefully selects the content, students will study topics for which they already possess schemata (i.e., the relevant linguistic, content, and cultural background knowledge): for example, geography, the arts, history, society, and literature. Using content and context together to understand messages, students develop copying mechanisms for dealing with unknown language in other context, ultimately fostering the development of foreign language proficiency. (8–9)

Yet teachers sometimes feel daunted when giving materials prepared for native speakers to students who are at proficiency levels of 2 or lower. A typical teacher reaction is, "This material is too advanced for my students!" In this situation, the challenge to the teacher is to create a linguistically simple but cognitively challenging task that is at once realistic and interesting to the students. (297)

CBI-trained teachers, then, do not set out to find web materials with a high frequency of certain linguistic structures—which is the objective of the grammar-in-context approach—but rather to identify topics that allow L2 learners to reflect on their L1 and L2 knowledge base (i.e., existing schemata) in new and illuminating ways. What would be an algorithm for creating a CBI lesson? The following procedures might be one way to get started within a web-based learning environment:

- Identify a topic of interest from the perspective of both the goals of the curriculum and the present knowledge of the L2 learners.[9]
- Find a brief web passage dealing with that topic (copyright laws must be observed!).[10]
- Add sound and glosses to the text.
- Provide brainstorming activities to activate semantic notions (i.e., schemata) about the topic in such a way as to bridge students' knowledge base to the new concepts found in the target culture.
- Design reading strategies and prereading tasks that address the difficulties associated with the selected reading passage.
- Instruct students to read and/or listen to the passage.
- Prepare comprehension questions.
- Design grammar tasks that ask students to do something with materials from the text, with the difficulty level dependent on the class level (the same reading passage can be repurposed for different levels): for example, (a) find nouns marked for feminine gender, (b) search for cognates, (c) change spoken citation or first-person verbs into indirect discourse, (d) rewrite the narrative using the past tense (i.e., using indirect discourse instead of direct discourse).
- Provide supplementary grammar explanations needed to support the assigned grammar task(s).
- Direct students to work in pairs to accomplish a real-world task related to the topic and grammar at hand.
- Incorporate the resources available on the web.
- Give students key words (pretested for successful results) to facilitate

their carrying out additional web searches related to the process of their collaborative task.
- Guide students to write an essay summarizing the results of their collaborative work.
- Instruct students how to make a presentation in class based on the results of their collaborate work.

Clearly, this is a generic, but not exhaustive, formula for creating CBI language materials supported by technology (also see Leaver and Willis 2004, and Jeon-Ellis, Debski, and Wigglesworth 2005 on the project-oriented classroom; Brandl 2002 on student-determined lessons; and Levine and Morse 2004 on global simulation German course).[11] Nor do CBI proponents advocate a fixed approach (Stryker and Leaver 1997, 3); each reading, video, or sound recording demands a fresh approach that depends on a unique interaction among the teacher, the students, and the authentic materials (what Meskill 2005 has called a triadic scaffold). CBI favors student control while allowing the instructor to establish a learning pathway so that students won't get lost.

Schaumann and Green (2004) have taken the idea of student control to heart and have developed an upper-division literature course for German in which their students create a web curriculum as a class project. Their students, like all L2 literature students, must first grapple with the difficulties presented by primary literature texts, then provide glosses, annotations, cultural and grammatical explanations, and background materials as an articulated set of web pages from which future classes can benefit. Selber (2004) calls this type of student-driven activity the cultivation of rhetorical computer literacy, a topic I return to in chapter 6.

Also notice that these suggestions—with the exception of doing web searches, playing web sound, and setting up pop-up textual glosses—could also be implemented in more traditional ways. The instructor need only find appropriate web materials (URLs); the rest of the lesson has to do with constructing a sound pedagogy around those materials, which is what teaching should be about. Some of the activities are done individually on the web outside of class as preparation (e.g., prereading activities, intensive reading, searching), and other tasks are carried out working in conjunction with a partner face-to-face. This is not to deny the attraction of putting all parts of the lesson on the web to take full advantage of the medium if the instructor has the knowledge, time, and patience to persevere. In chapter 4 I illustrate how even collaborative tasks such as those discussed previously can be done online using CMC tools.

DISCUSSION QUESTIONS AND ACTIVITIES

1. Find a web page in the language that you teach that you predict will help your students learn something important about the L2 language and culture. Create a lesson plan around this web page that can be carried out in a classroom setting. Include a set of learning objectives for your lesson and try to make your accompanying activities as student centered as possible. Consider ways in which your students would benefit from previewing guidance; what would they need to do to appreciate your selection? Share your web page with your colleagues and ask for reactions.

2. Revisit your lesson plan from question 1 and consider what you have to include in the way of online materials (e.g., text, images, sound, video, explanations, instructions) if students were to accomplish the stated learning objectives by working outside of class time, either by themselves or in groups.

3. Can pragmatics be taught online? Review *Dancing with Words: Strategies for Learning Pragmatics in Spanish* (Cohen and Sykes, 2006: www.carla.umn.edu/speechacts/sp_pragmatics/home.html). Is the overall presentation and design helpful for teaching pragmatics? Discuss the ways in which your students would react to using these web pages. If your language is one other than Spanish, imagine the effect that similar web pages in your language would have on your students. How could this approach be adapted to the language and the level that you teach?

4. Use Microsoft Word to produce a simple web page for your students (perhaps a presentation of the rationale or goals for taking one of your courses). Be sure to save it by choosing the option <Save as web page>. View your page with your favorite browser and share the results with a colleague or your class for comments and suggestions.

5.   According to Laurillard (2002, 93), web pages such as the ones you researched in connection with question 1 are best suited for presenting and working with narratives. If that is true, discuss why you will need to adopt a CBI approach for using web pages to be successful teaching specific cultural or grammar points using these web pages.

NOTES

1. The authors of the Pew report also caution that 13 percent of American teenagers (3 million), characterized by their lower levels of income and/or African American ethnicity, still do not use the Internet. This could potentially feed a digital divide with insidious effects for our society (for a different perspective on this topic, see Warschauer 2002; Warschauer, Knobel, and Stone 2004; Crump and McIlroy 2003).
2. Global Reach (2004) reports that 36 percent of the world's Internet users process their access in English, but these statistics were collected in 2004.
3. More information on the terms and concepts used in the following sections can be found online at Wikipedia, at http://en.wikipedia.org/.
4. Arocena's HTML manual, written in Spanish, is the best practical guide to learn how to write code that I have seen in any language.
5. For links lists by individuals, see, for example, Tennessee Bob's Famous French links, www.utm.edu/departments/french/french.html; for lists by university language labs, see the Yamada Language Center, http://babel.uoregon.edu/.
6. See www.cortland.edu/flteach/flteach-res.html.
7. Ironically, Chun also reported at the CALICO 2002 conference that when students were free to choose, they preferred simple English-translation glosses without video or sound. Chun found (personal communication) that these different strategies were not correlated with academic performance. The data from Karp's (2002) unpublished dissertation also demonstrated learner preference for English-translation glosses over multimedia ones.
8. I include under this rubric task-based instruction (cf. Ellis 2003), project-based instruction, and inquiry-based learning as well, although each name is intended to highlight special procedural features. A top-down method puts meaning first, in contrast to a bottom-up method, which begins by decoding morphemes, words, phrases, sentences, and so on.
9. The University of California, Santa Cruz, Spanish program offers a first-year sequence based on topics within a CBI framework. María Victoria González Pagani developed the course concept and materials. She also authored CBI web materials for *Al corriente* (Blake, González Pagani, Ramos, and Marks 2003) and was the co–principal investigator (co-PI) for *Spanish without Walls* (Blake and Delforge 2005), a Spanish distance-learning course produced with support from FIPSE (P116B000315).

10. The University of Texas system offers sound advice on copyright, fair use, and multimedia: www.utsystem.edu/ogc/intellectualproperty/multimed.htm. The FLTEACH site also has good copyright information: www.cortland.edu/flteach/mm-course/copyright.html.
11. For one instantiation of this paradigm with respect to intermediate Spanish instruction, see María Victoria González Pagani's web pages for *Al corriente* (Blake, González Pagani, Ramos, and Marks 2003): http://highered.mcgraw-hill.com/sites/0072496401/student_view0/.

Chapter 3

CALL and Its Evaluation

A HISTORY OF CALL

As discussed in chapter 2, the impact of the Internet is the central focus of CALL because of its prominent role in today's FL classroom and in the lives of the students. However, the first applications of computer technology in the field of FL teaching were implemented in the 1960s on mainframe computers within a Skinnerian behaviorist framework where learning a language meant memorizing a body of well-choreographed responses that included frequent vocabulary items, clichés, and phrases used at appropriate moments in a conversation. Accordingly, language teaching was viewed as a type of conditioning, getting students to produce a series of responses in reaction to particular stimuli (i.e., stimulus/response theory). Not surprising given the political reaction caused by the Sputnik launch, the first computer language programs developed at Stanford University, Dartmouth College, and the University of Essex exclusively dealt with Russian language instruction (Beatty 2003, 17–18). These mainframe programs were linear in nature and patterned after the activities typically found in language workbooks. This approach is often referred to as *computer-assisted language instruction (CALI, or language CAI)*, in contrast to *computer-assisted language learning (CALL)*, where the latter term implies an approach more in line with the notions of communicative competence and the negotiation of meaning in a nonbehaviorist framework. Computer-Assisted Language Instruction Consortium (CALICO), the name of the main professional organization dedicated to studying technology and language, still bears the original CALI acronym.

The most extreme form of language CAI is derogatorily labeled as drill-and-kill. This is not to say that the CAI approach of programmed instruction has no value for language learning or that it does not produce any student outcomes. Rather this approach assumes that the mastery of any given subject matter results directly from a cumulative investment of time and practice applied to a learning object that can be broken into subunits and arranged in a linear fashion (Lai and Biggs 1994, 13). Many SLA theorists would argue that perfect mastery (i.e., becoming a NS) is not a realistic goal for L2 learners (Bley-Vroman 1990) and that language cannot be treated as a collection of linearly organized subunits (i.e., learn *a*, then *b*, then *c*, etc.). However, the fact that drill-and-kill exercises are still widely used proves, at the very least, that some FL professions still believe them to be of value for L2 learners in certain circumstances—for instance, for learning heavily inflected verb morphology systems such as Russian.

Alternately, Delcloque (2001, 69) refers to the 1960s and 1970s as the text phase in the history of CALL, where "much of the pioneering work . . . involved the manipulation of text on screen." There was also a preoccupation with making foreign-character fonts work on the computer, a topic that has been completely surpassed by the advent of Unicode, a universal protocol for assigning ASCII values to the letters found in more than 250 of the world's languages.[1]

This period also encompasses the groundbreaking efforts carried out in the 1960s at the University of Illinois with the PLATO project (Programmed Logic/Learning for Automated Teaching Operations; Beatty 2003, 18). Despite its reliance on a grammar translation approach—and again, Russian dominated the early focus of the PLATO project—this pre-DOS CAI program offered students an amazing variety of computer language activities dealing with vocabulary, grammar, and translations that took more than seventy hours for students to complete. These materials also provided students both corrective and diagnostic feedback, spell checkers, and grammar checkers.

The 1980s marked the initiation of a new platform, Macintosh (released in 1984), along with its *GUI* or *graphical user interface* and a general switch from mainframe computers to microcomputers. Macintosh's HyperCard application also introduced the new concept of hypertext, a nonlinear way of organizing multimedia materials, information, and activities that broke the CAI linear mold and launched a new generation of computer programs that now could be referred to as CALL (Delcloque 2001, 69). Microcomputers were also driving (i.e., "giving instructions to") laserdisc players and, in time, the more compact and convenient medium of CD-ROMs and DVDs, with a large capacity for multimedia (e.g., video, audio, graphics, images, and text) that could be accessed randomly using digital technology. The earliest nonlinear programs developed at Brigham Young University (BYU)—*Macario, Montevidisco,* and *Dígame* (Gale 1989)—used laserdisc technology to simulate adventures in a Spanish-speaking country and force students to become involved in the storyline by making choices that branched off in different directions. The descriptor *interactive* truly seemed to apply to this type of software.

Following fast on BYU's footsteps, a group of researchers at MIT embarked on the Athena Language Learning Project (ALLP) and produced three laserdisc simulations of exceptional quality, mimicking real-world tasks based on meaning and authentic materials: *À la rencontre de Phillippe, Dans le Quartier Saint-Gervais,* and *No Recuerdo* (Murray, Morgenstern, and Furstenberg 1989). These simulations provided multiple protagonists, multiple plots, knowledge-based choices, surprises, multimedia presentations, and an intrinsic motivation to complete the materials.[2] These stimulations were originally programmed for the UNIX platform, which never translated gracefully to the microcomputer environment with CD-ROMs (instead of laserdiscs) so as to be widely used by the FL profession. Nor did the *authoring tools* of the time (i.e., HyperCard) provide the necessary robustness to duplicate the original performance afforded by the UNIX system. Still, these programs stand as a pillar of CALL creativity because they emphasized meaning over endless repetition of forms.

In both the BYU and MIT cases, the programming and video production costs for these projects required a sizable institutional investment along with additional governmental support. Few individual teachers or CALL developers found themselves in such favorable circumstances. In the meantime, in the classroom trenches, many more modest efforts to produce in-house CALL programs for the microcomputing environment were being pursued by language teachers using relatively transparent authoring tools such as HyperCard (Mac), Tool Book (PC), Libra (Mac/PC), and WinCalis (PC), just to name a few. These technical advances coincide with what Delcloque (2001, 70) calls the CD-ROM and authoring tool phases of CALL. The ability to produce do-it-yourself programs generated considerable interest in CALL from among the rank and file, which was a very good thing.

Commercial entities also began to produce what Levy (1997, 178–214) has dubbed tutorial CALL programs (with or without CD-ROMs) for consumption in this new microcomputing world. Tutorial CALL is a more friendly way to refer to language CAI programmed instruction, where the computer guides the learner and, hopefully, offers feedback along the way. The CALICO Review is an excellent source for evaluating existing commercial language software, as is the FLTEACH website.[3] Publishing houses began to invest in multimedia programs, as well, usually delivered on CD-ROMs and intended as a complement to help sell their books (see Jones 1999).

Feedback and artificial intelligence also became a new focus for what was called *iCALL* (i.e., intelligent CALL). Previously, the behaviorist model had viewed students as a blank slate and consequently tried to stimulate them to produce correct answers by using a very controlled sequencing of the learning materials. But what should a computer program do when the learner fails to reach the expected outcome, despite the controlled stimuli of the programmed instruction? Inevitably students are going to make mistakes along the way—lots of mistakes. What feedback or directions will they receive from the CALL program at these junctures? In contrast to the CALI phase, the new CALL paradigm assumes that students bring certain schemata to the learning process. Consequently, a well-designed CALL program should engage learners in problem-solving activities or constructivism in order to make use of each learner's previous experiences. To accomplish this, the program must guide students by giving feedback. This is easier said than done if the feedback must be customized to each learner, the obvious ideal. Providing error correction that is more complex than "right/wrong/here's the answer/try again" is not a simple programming proposition.

To begin with, computer scientists have hotly debated what constitutes computer intelligence. Alan Turing (1950) argued in the early 1950s that if you cannot discern that you are interacting with a machine then the program is intelligent. To add fuel to this debate, Weizenbaum (1966) wrote a simple *chatterbot* program in 1966 called *Eliza* that mimicked through textual exchanges the behavior of a psychiatrist. The program gives the appearance of being a sympathetic listener who prods the user with follow-up questions such as "How are you feeling?" "Why are you feeling tired? "Tell me more of last night." In actual fact, the program matches key phrases, nouns, adjectives, verbs, and adverbs recognized only as character strings (i.e., not as parsed linguistic structures) and then matches these strings with clichéd responses that give the impression of a normal, give-and-take conversation. The basic programming was later adapted for German (PSYCHIATER and SCION) and Spanish (FAMILIA; see Underwood 1984, 75–79, and 1989; for online examples, see Fryer and Carpenter 2006).[4] *Eliza* and other chatterbot programs are amusing to students in the short run but hardly what they need in the long run in order to develop their L2 competence. I return to the issue of iCALL and feedback in greater detail later.

What is clear, however, is that for most CALL practitioners and users the level of feedback is closely tied to the program's level of interactivity and its ability to allow the learner more autonomy to direct the discovery process. Kern and Warschauer (2000), among other researchers, use the word "agency" to describe this educational goal. They argue that the ideal CALL activity is one that encourages the L2 learner to become an agent in the learning process. Accordingly, they analyze CALL history in terms of pedagogical advances rather than technological innovations such as those described earlier (i.e., mainframe computers, microcomputers, laserdiscs, CD-ROMs, the web), as illustrated in table 3.1. Integrative CALL, the third phase, includes activities in which people interact with other people via the computer, which is the topic of the next chapter (CMC). In turn, the study of CMC motivates the need to discuss issues concerning sociocultural or intercultural competences, which are also covered in the next chapter.

CALL AND THE PROFESSION

Academics working in CALL have only gradually experienced professional acceptance and recognition of their efforts. In general, applied fields always seem to struggle in academia for validation when compared with entrenched notions of what constitutes real academic work, and the case of CALL is no different. Fortunately professional organizations such as CALICO, the Modern Language Association (MLA), and EUROCALL agree quite closely on what constitutes the field of CALL and what academic value this type of work should have in terms of career advancement. It is noteworthy that the American Association for Applied Linguistics (AAAL), which hosts one of the première SLA annual conferences, regularly

Table 3.1   The Three Stages of CALL

Stage	1970s–1980s: Structural CALL	1980s–1990s: Communicative CALL	Twenty-first Century: Integrative CALL
Technology	Mainframe	PCs	Multimedia and Internet
Teaching paradigm	Grammar translation and audio-lingual	Communicative language teaching	Content-based instruction
View of language	Structural (a formal structural system)	Cognitive (a mentally constructed system)	Sociocognitive (developed in social interaction)
Principal use of computers	Drill and practice	Communicative exercises	Authentic discourse
Principal objective	Accuracy	Fluency	Agency

Source: Adapted from Kern and Warschauer 2000.

includes a strand dealing with language and technology. In other words, the CALL field is considered part of SLA studies, with all the privileges and responsibilities to do sound research (Chapelle 2005).

CALICO and EUROCALL issued a joint statement in 1999 on CALL research that carefully situates the field within an SLA context.[5] These organizations consider that CALL work can include research, development, and/or practice. While carefully distinguishing among these three aspects of CALL work, the CALICO and EUROCALL membership also stress that they often overlap.

> Research may be separate from development, in that a researcher may explore the effects of using technology-based tools or materials developed by others, e.g. formative evaluations, or may focus entirely on theory development. In CALL the progression often begins with pedagogical practice or learner needs driving the development of technology-based materials, techniques, or environments. This development effort may then later lead to research, which in turn may or may not be used to generate theoretical implications. Nonetheless, in

establishing criteria for evaluating CALL work for purposes of academic recognition and reward, it is important that the distinctions between these activities be clearly articulated.[6]

The MLA's policy statement on CALL research focuses more on the contractual issues surrounding someone engaged in CALL development: In other words, will they be judged fairly in their careers by their colleagues in the humanities?[7] The MLA policy suggests that academics doing CALL research, development, and practice should negotiate and validate these activities at the time of employment so that misunderstandings will not arise later in the personnel process. The MLA statement also acknowledges the changing nature of this field and the need to temper traditional perceptions about scholarship, especially when based on research only done in literature: "Academic work in digital media should be evaluated in the light of these rapidly changing institutional and professional contexts, and departments should recognize that some traditional notions of scholarship, teaching, and service are being redefined."[8]

Clearly academics doing CALL work need to be reviewed by their peers, other academics involved in the CALL field, especially given the abrupt changes or phases outlined earlier that have occurred in a relatively short time period. The next section returns to tutorial CALL, lest the reader come away with the impression that the CALL field is dominated only by ideas about enabling learner agency, CMC, and/or sociocultural competence.

TUTORIAL CALL

Levy (1997) and Hubbard and Bradin Siskin (2004) distinguish between the computer as tutor and the computer as tool, for instance, in support of human interactions and CMC activities. In the former case, the computer controls the learning and automatically evaluates the students' responses while the instructor seemingly has little or no role. Hubbard and Bradin Siskin suggest that this conception of CALL harkens back to old CALL or what I have called the CAI phase. They question whether or not this separation between old versus new CALL must necessarily be the case. Why can't a FL curriculum employ both types of CALL to advantage? Clearly students with relatively low levels of linguistic competence in L2 need more guidance such as might be offered by a tutorial CALL program (Bertin 2001). In chapter 5 I explore a case study of a distance learning course for L2 Spanish where both tutorial CALL and the computer as tool are employed to advance different purposes at different times in the online course *Spanish without Walls*. For the moment, let us focus in the next section on one specific usage of tutorial CALL that everyone accepts and even expects from CALL materials: vocabulary glossing.

The Case of Vocabulary Glosses for L2 Reading

The FL profession needs no convincing with respect to the importance of reading authentic materials in order to stimulate L2 development. Krashen (2004) now considers reading to be of fundamental importance for moving ahead with advanced proficiency and academic language skills; he routinely campaigns in the schools in favor of setting aside time during class for free voluntary reading. But for the L2 student, the lack of both vocabulary breadth and depth remains a formidable obstacle to reading authentic materials, especially because most unfamiliar words, excluding the high-frequency functors (i.e., words with only a grammatical function but little referential meaning) that make the grammar work, are used only once or twice in a given passage (Knight 1994).

An online program such as WordChamp (for a review, see LeLoup and Ponterio 2005) presents one free software solution to this problem by allowing users to paste in FL texts or enter the URLs.[9] WordChamp then analyzes the passage and highlights the words it has in its database, allowing the user to roll the cursor over a word and receive a gloss and, if available, an audio recording of its pronunciation. WordChamp offers an option to add new words to the user's flash card list to be practiced at another session. Word-Champ makes available this service in an amazing number of languages, but not every language database has extensive audio recordings to accompany the word definitions (see Arabic, for example). Ultralingua.net (LeLoup and Ponterio 2005) is a similar software program that uses pop-up windows instead of the rollover cursor, but it only covers the major European languages.

Multimedia glossing has been the focus of much CALL research (for an excellent overview, see Chun 2006). According to Chun (2006, 78), L2 vocabulary is best remembered when learners look up picture or video glosses in addition to receiving translations of unfamiliar words. But if given the choice, L2 learners tend to choose only simple translations. Chun's (2006, 82) study shows that lexical knowledge, rather than grammatical knowledge, is significantly related to both reading and listening comprehension. Following Grabe's work (2004), Chun correctly points out two separate aspects of lexical knowledge that impact reading comprehension: the learning of vocabulary and the fluency (i.e., automaticity) of word recognition. The research shows that explicit instruction, including tutorial CALL (see Lafford, Lafford, and Sykes 2007), has a significant impact on vocabulary acquisition, but reading comprehension is more complicated and is affected by a number of factors, especially prior or background knowledge of the material to be read. As was suggested in chapter 2 with respect to preparing web activities, Chun (2006, 92) counsels teachers to include a large battery of prereading activities in order to prime students for what they will encounter.

Note that glossing programs such as WordChamp combine both user and computer control in ways that blur the distinctions between tutorial CALL and tool CALL. The user is fully in control of which words are looked up, but the size and complexity of the database determine what stimuli the reader has available and in what form, multimedia or not. Fukkink, Hulstijn, and Simis (2005) have demonstrated that L2 students retrieve faster and with less variation the unfamiliar words on which they have trained in contrast to those on which they have not trained. Research of this kind indicates obvious areas where tutorial CALL and explicit instruction can make a difference in L2 development. In the next section, I explore simple authoring systems that allow teachers to create their own tutorial CALL programs with modest investments of time and resources.

Authoring Tools

At the height of the CALL platform wars (Mac vs. PC) that took place in the 1980s, the CALL field was searching for the perfect authoring template, a program that would allow nonprogrammers, which is the case for most FL teachers, the ability to create CALL exercises with relative ease (Garrett 1991). Davies (2006, module 2.5) provides a list of only some of the authoring tools from that period and just beyond that have vied for the distinction of the ideal CALL template—although most of them are now obsolete:

> TES/T, Pilot, COMET, CAN, WatCAN, CALIS, WinCALIS, Dasher, Edutext, Microtext, Tutor, TenCore, Course of Action, Storyboard, CopyWrite, Quartext, WordPlay, TextPlay, Developing Tray, Question Mark, ClozeWrite, Clozemaster, UNIT, Gapfil, Speedread, ToolBook, HyperCard, HyperStudio, MediaLink, QuestNet, IconAuthor, CBT Express, Course Builder, Guide, HyperShell, Linkway, BonAccord, Partner Tools, Learning Space, Authorware, Director.

Delcloque (2001, 71) adds a few more authoring tools from the 1980s and 1990s to this list: LAVAC, Libra, MacLang, SuperMacLang, Speaker, and SuperCard. In addition, another group of platform-specific authoring tools, all with different pricing schemes, includes the following: Author Plus (PC), Authoring Suite/Wida Software (PC, includes Storyboard), Blue-GLAS (PC), and MaxAuthor (PC).[10] Hot Potatoes provides an interface for both operating systems that can be exported to the web (and is free for educators). Increasingly so, authoring tools are web-based applications, avoiding the pesky issues of cross-platform compatibility altogether: Interactive Language Learning Authoring Package (web-based), ExTemplate (web-based), Swarthmore Makers (web-based), Marmo Marmo's JavaScript templates (web-based), Yale's Center for Language Study Comet templates (web-based), and CLEAR's SMILE templates (web-based).[11] This generalization extends to learning/class management systems (*LMS/CMS*) such as WebCT, Blackboard, and Moodle.

Using a template to develop CALL activities enormously simplifies the development phase, but it also tends to constrain the creator to a predetermined set of formats such as multiple choice, fill in the blank, drag and drop, click text/image on screen, and the like. In general, the student feedback produced by these authoring tools is also limited to string recognition.

In the 1990s, the University of Victoria sponsored the development of a set of templates that came to be known as Hot Potatoes that is now distributed free for educators by Half-Baked Software.[12] The Hot Potatoes software consists of a suite of six cross-platform templates (for Mac OS X, Windows, Linux, or any computer running a Java Virtual Machine) that has stood the test of time and heavy use by language teachers. The different templates allow FL teachers to create multiple-choice exercises, word-entry exercises (single word, phrase, string, or open-ended), crossword puzzles, cloze (fill-in) exercises, jumble-word exercises, and mix-and-match exercises (Winke and MacGregor 2001). All types of activities can be published as a stand-alone PC or Mac application or as a web document. Both interface and some of the feedback routines can be customized along with adding a CGI hook to store the results or scores in a designated server available to the course instructors. The current versions are fully Unicode compliant.

When several templates or functions are bundled into one seamless development package, along with more advanced multimedia capabilities, then one can speak of an authoring system such as Authorware and Director (and Flash for delivery of animations and multimedia), familiar names from Davies's list that have survived into the twenty-first century. Authoring systems require significantly more programming experience and have steep learning curves. Teachers are well served to seek out technical support with these authoring systems from their respective institutions. Nevertheless, with the right technical support, authoring systems help to produce CALL programs that are sophisticated even at the commercial level. Jim Duber's website offers a series of English-language demos of what these technologies can accomplish for the teacher.[13]

Following the current trend to make everything web-based, LMSs such as WebCT, Blackboard, or Moodle (Brandl 2005) offer a template-based system already built into a course framework. Godwin-Jones (2003b, 18) extols the virtues of LMSs for distance learning, because "an LMS can supply crucial communication and management tools, as well as assessment builders and grade book functionality." Again, Godwin-Jones correctly states that "LMS excel at course and user management but they are not strong in content creation." This fact sometimes forces the teacher to develop the content outside of the LMS and then link these materials to the LMS shell. But both Blackboard and WebCT are beginning to open up their proprietary systems to accommodate plug-ins and add-ons in order to extend the functionality while retaining the familiar LMS user interface.

FEEDBACK, iCALL, AND AUTOMATIC SPEECH
RECOGNITION (ASR)

One of the key concerns about tutorial CALL revolves around the notion of interactivity: How responsive and adaptive (or rather, effective) can computers be to students' needs at the discursive level? Laurillard (2002, 118) is right to caution us about the limits of providing discursive feedback:

> The responsiveness of the interactive medium is limited, however. Hypermedia environments, enhanced or otherwise, are not adaptive to the student's needs at either the discursive or the interactive level. It would not be possible for the student to tell if they had made an inappropriate interpretation of the resources, as the system remains neutral and unvarying with respect to anything they do. . . . [T]here is no way of the student being able to test whether their interpretation is correct, except by comparing it with the various expert views then made available in the form of model answers.

In the earlier days of CALL, feedback focused more on the grammatical or sentence level. CALL feedback was limited to spell checkers, grammar checkers, and discrete string or keyword matching. Unfortunately, most spell checkers assume that the users are already competent speakers of that language. Few programs are designed with L2 learners in mind, who exhibit an emerging linguistic competence referred to as interlanguage (for an example of this problem, see Burston's 1998 review of a French spell checker). Spellcheckers do well at catching single letter violations but often fail to analyze learners' more competence-based errors (Heift and Schulze 2007, 166–67).

While string-matching routines, such as what is available from Hot Potatoes, are far better than simple right/wrong responses—oftentimes further exacerbated by punctuation demands in some applications (i.e., a correct answer could be considered incorrect if the period is missing)—this approach still falls short of providing students with CALL materials that can truly be labeled as interactive. As the CALL field has moved away from the model of drill-and-kill tutorials, the field has demanded CALL applications that react to student input in ways that appeared to be more context sensitive. As early as the 1980s, Underwood (1989) described what the ideal intelligent tutoring system (ITS) should be able to do: act as a real tutor or guardian for L2 students, leading them by the hand to discover more and more about the target language with each response and prescribing the appropriate exercises and metalinguistic explanations about the language that are needed to advance. An ITS, then, involves an expert (usually, some type of grammatical parser, a program capable of separating utterances into phrases, words, parts of speech, and limited semantic interpretations), a student, and a teacher module, frequently circumscribed in a highly defined semantic microworld, or domain, in order to minimize potential ambiguities and confusion. At the time, artificial intelligence (AI), a subfield of computer science, held great promise that something like Underwood's forward-looking description of an expert tutor could actually come to pass.

Gradually the term ITS, or "expert system," was supplanted by iCALL, or intelligent CALL, but as Schulze (2001) explains, a more accurate name would be "parser-based CALL." This later term makes it clear that natural language parsers are used to evaluate students' syntactic and sometimes semantic input. While Schulze (2001, 117) openly acknowledges that a parser-based CALL cannot account for the full complexity of natural human languages, "it does not mean that interesting fragments or aspects of a given language cannot be captured by a formal linguistic theory and hence implemented in a CALL application."[14] Obviously, a parser-based approach places an inordinate emphasis on morpho-syntactic errors—not a bad thing seeing that these types of errors appear to constitute the most frequently occurring mistakes that students make in freely produced texts (Schulze 2001, 121; Juozulynas 1994). However, the parser approach also produces its share of false acceptances and false alarms. The more constrained the semantic domain is, the more successful the parser will be at diagnosing errors.

Much more serious for the iCALL field has been the fact that despite a great deal of work in AI over the years, there still exist only two operational web-based iCALL programs: E-Tutor for German (Heift 2002; Heift and Schulze 2007) and Robo-Sensei for Japanese (formerly called Banzai; Nagata 1993, 1995, 2002; for a review, see Ushida 2007).[15] A third system, Tagarela for Portuguese, was recently introduced at Ohio State University. The goal of all these programs is to provide error-specific feedback and flexibility in handling student textual input.

In the case of the E-Tutor, a natural language parser for German is combined with a student module that tracks each student's errors and proficiency level, controlling the type of feedback that will be delivered: namely, for beginners and intermediates, rich metalinguistic feedback messages and remedial exercises (e.g., dictation, build a phrase, which word is different, word order practice, build a sentence) but something much less explicit for advanced users who need only light guidance.

Heift (2001) acknowledges that building this type of parser-based CALL is very labor and time intensive and requires close cooperation among computer programmers, linguists, and pedagogues. However, error analysis of this ilk can also be very accurate in providing the type of feedback and interactivity that is helpful to the learner, even if it does not meet the lofty ideals that Underwood (1989) originally imagined. And students really pay attention to well-crafted feedback. Heift (2002) discovered that most students (85%) using E-Tutor revised their sentences without peeking at the answers, with the weaker performers tending to also be the more frequent peekers. Heift (2004) has also shown that the more explicit and metalinguistic in nature the feedback is, the more it helps the L2 learners successfully complete their L2 tasks.

Why, then, has iCALL not gained more notice in the CALL field? Perhaps what has distracted the field from the slow but sure advances in parser-based error analysis has been the meteoric surge of interest in CMC and sociocultural/intercultural research, the subject of the next chapter. In short, CALL practitioners are looking at human communication as the true source of interactivity. However, much learning still occurs when individuals are alone, working by themselves in isolation at odd times and places. In these self-study times, iCALL has proven superior to using static workbooks alone (Nagata 1996). When one considers that classroom teachers infrequently correct phonological and grammatical errors but rather concentrate on discourse, content, and lexical errors (Ellis 1994, 585), iCALL could have an honored niche in the L2 learner's individual study time. As more parser-based systems become available for a large array of languages, iCALL still holds considerable promise as a useful tool for L2 learning.

Feedback to textual input is not the only kind of response the computer is capable of. While iCALL has concentrated on syntax and text production, researchers working on *automatic speech recognition (ASR)* have looked to applying their results to teach pronunciation. As in the case of parsers, ASR applications "perform best when designed to operate in clearly circumscribed linguistic sub-domains" (Ehsani and Knodt 1998, 56), in pursuit of executing specific tasks: for example, individual sound practice, word recognition, and short sentence repetition.

Ehsani and Knodt (1998, 56) assert that the most common approach to implementing ASR involves developing (a) an acoustic signal analyzer that computes a spectral representation of incoming speech; (b) a set of sound or phonemic models based on sophisticated probabilistic computations called hidden Markov modeling and, then, further trained by a large corpus of actual speech; (c) a lexicon for converting phones into words; (d) a statistically based grammar that defines legitimate word combinations at the sentence level; and (e) a decoder that makes the best match between the sound and a corresponding word string. Building such a system requires a large amount of speech data from speakers of different accents and conditions (i.e., while reading or producing spontaneous speech). Adapting it for L2 learners requires additional training of the system using large corpora of nonnative speech data from learners of varying degrees of proficiency.

Ehsani and Knodt (1998, 60) caution that delimiting the performance domain or task is one of the most important steps in designing a successful ASR application. While ASR software is good at recognizing short utterances (words, phrases, or short sentences), continuous spoken language input with open responses and multiturn dialogs poses almost insurmountable challenges without access to powerful computers and lots of memory. In addition, the input must be clear and noise free, which often depends on a good microphone and noise-cancellation baffle.

Despite these obstacles, commercial software does exist that provides specific exercises dealing with mastering linguistic forms at the word or sentence level as opposed to simulating real communicative exchanges. For instance, Tell Me More Pro (Auralog; for a review of the Spanish version, see Lafford 2004)[16] tracks and visually displays the waveform and pitch contours from speech input in nine languages and compares them to those patterned after NS; the program then scores the learner's efforts on a scale from 1 to 7. The learner can zero in and practice particular phones in isolation, if so desired. *Tell Me More* also provides a 3-D animation that demonstrates how the lips and tongue should move to produce the target sound.

With the Auralog sentence exercises, L2 learners choose to speak one of several closed responses with ready-made vocabulary and syntax, which greatly simplifies the speech recognition algorithm but prohibits learners from actively constructing their own utterances (Eskenazi 1999, 64). As Eskenazi (1999, 64–65) observes, "To our knowledge, current speech-interactive language tutors do not let learners freely create their own utterances because underlying speech recognizers require a high degree of predictability to perform reliably." Eskenazi (1999) and Eskenazi and Brown (2006) report on some successful research efforts (i.e., the FLUENCY project and the Sphinx-2 project at Carnegie Mellon University) to construct a production task that uses carefully constrained elicitation techniques (patterned after the MLA's audio-lingual method) to guide the L2 learners into speaking only the specifically targeted speech data.

ASR technology, as in the case of parser-based iCALL, may have a significant impact on CALL development in the near future, but what the field needs now is an authoring tool that makes incorporating ASR simple for nonengineers. Undoubtedly this will be forthcoming soon, but more serious obstacles to implementing ASR in any given language will be the existence of and access to large corpora of native and nonnative speech data, in both written and conversational formats.

CALL EVALUATION

Understandably, not every language teacher will actively wish to launch into the creation of technologically based materials for their students, but everyone should be interested in evaluating CALL materials in service of the FL curriculum. Just as with the myriad of textbook choices in the FL marketplace, FL teachers have a professional responsibility to seek out and select what they consider to be the best set of CALL learning materials for their students. But evaluating CALL software is no longer the straightforward endeavor that it might have been in the 1960s, as Levy and Stockwell (2006, chap. 3) take pains to point out (also see Bickerton, Stenton, and Temmerman 2001). Current techniques range from using checklists to more complicated longitudinal evaluation studies involving the collection of both qualitative and quantitative data (Levy and Stockwell 2006, 40).

In the first place, the CALL field has expanded to include not only tutorial CAI programs but also web pages, CD-ROMs, DVDs, and computer-mediated activities such as chat. The variety of CALL programs and activities should not all be evaluated in the same way, because they have different purposes and ask students to achieve different goals. Likewise, software evaluation needs to be considered separately from the more general SLA research questions dealing with the effects and/or effectiveness of CALL (for more on research issues, see Burston 2006). Typically, CALL software evaluation emphasizes design issues, activity procedures, or theoretical and/or methodological approaches.

Checklists and surveys, usually based on a Likert scale (i.e., numerical ratings from 1 to 5, with 1 being "strongly disagree" and 5 being "strongly agree"), with room for additional comments, overwhelmingly focus on design issues and probably constitute the most widely used method for evaluating CALL materials. The Information and Communications Technology for Language Teachers Project (ICT4LT; see Davies 2006), sponsored by the Commission of the European Communities and the EUROCALL organization, provides a handy CALL evaluation checklist, which is downloadable from their website.[17] This checklist offers a series of queries dealing with the L2 language level, the user interface and navigational issues, the use of multimedia (e.g., video, photos, graphics, animation, sound), the provision of help and/or feedback, the level of interactivity, and the availability of performance scoring. Checklists are a good place to start but often restrict the evaluation process to technical and design factors.

A more involved evaluation framework, the CALICO Journal, maintains an excellent online software review section, edited by Burston (2003).[18] Instead of checklists or surveys, the *CALICO Journal* asks their reviewers to examine the critical properties of the CALL materials in question, focusing on pedagogical validity, adaptability to different learning environments, efficiency, effectiveness (as judged by student outcomes), and innovation. Burston (2003) advocates using a set of eclectic criteria that combine the best of Hubbard's (2006) methodological approach and Chapelle's (2001) interactionist SLA framework.

Hubbard (1996, 2006) is most concerned with the right fit of the CALL software to the teacher's instructional approach. Hubbard (1996) highlights factors such as the teacher fit (methodological approach), the learner fit (as a function of the individual learner profiles, interests, and computer infrastructure), and the operational/procedural fit (interface features and activities types). Both Burston and Hubbard's concerns dictate the following guide to software evaluation, which is the basic format for all of the *CALICO Journal* reviews:

1. Technical preview
2. Operational description (activities and procedures)
3. Learner fit
4. Teacher fit

The reviewer (and consumer) must then decide what implementation schemes will be needed to integrate the reviewed CALL materials into the curriculum and, finally, make appropriateness judgments as to whether or not there is a good match between learner fit and teacher fit.

Chapelle (2001) is more concerned with the teacher fit in the sense of what the teacher assumes about how language is learned. Accordingly, her model provides an evaluation framework that is more SLA theory driven. The central concept in her model is the language-learning potential or the extent to which the CALL materials under review produce FonF and meaningful language negotiation, the very foundation of the interactionist theory reviewed in chapter 1. Chapelle judges all CALL materials as if they are activities or tasks with a positive or negative potential to stimulate learners to engage in language negotiations. For Chapelle, the appropriateness judgments deal with six factors: language-learning potential, learner fit, meaning focus, authenticity, positive impact (i.e., the effect on developing learning strategies, pragmatic abilities, and cultural awareness), and, finally, practicality. Given Chapelle's emphasis on FonF, it is not immediately obvious how to use this framework to evaluate CALL materials that focus solely on pronunciation, vocabulary, or discourse. Likewise, Levy and Stockwell (2006, 76) correctly note that too much is being grouped under the rather vague heading of positive impact ("the positive effects of the CALL activity on those who participate in it"). Linking an evaluation framework to a specific SLA theory is something of a doubled-edged sword: It increases specificity, which is good, but limits what will be looked at and subsequently valued.

In summary, CALL evaluation may examine design, procedures, approaches, or a combination of all of these factors. Clearly, the evaluation process has been complicated by the changing nature of what constitutes

CALL materials. While general frameworks such as Hubbard's and Chapelle's stimulate important avenues for evaluation, the specific goals of how an institution is using a given CALL program may require formulating a criteria based on the local learning environments and concerns. In a word, CALL evaluation is and should always be sensitive to context.

SUMMARY

Like the technology and the tools themselves, the notion of CALL has changed rapidly since its beginnings with the PLATO system in the 1960s. The field has evolved from notions such as tutorial programs and technology used as tools to accomplish learning tasks to a more integrated phase that emphasizes discursive and intercultural competence. Earlier concerns about how to type international fonts and drill morphology have fallen away to reveal a more sophisticated preoccupation with how to get students to develop a new and more bilingual sense of L2 cultural competence. Learning morphology and grammar has not disappeared, but rather teachers are endeavoring to put this learning in its proper place within the overall L2 curriculum. Accordingly, each type of CALL program and activity has its own place and time, as should be revealed by any thoughtful CALL evaluation process. Language teachers should be fully involved in evaluating CALL materials, even if they do not produce them—it is part of their profession.

Recently the CALL field has experienced a surge of interest in CMC, whether in real or deferred time. This social activity is immensely appealing to students and teachers alike as soon as they have enough vocabulary and structure to carrying this off, which is the topic of the next chapter. CMC research and practice has also been stimulated by a heightened awareness of the properties of discursive language and the need for students to develop intercultural competence (IC).

DISCUSSION QUESTIONS AND ACTIVITIES

1. Make a list of the pros and cons of using drill-and-kill types of CALL exercises.

2.   Write a definition for what the word *agency* means in relation to CALL.

3.   Download Hot Potatoes (it's free for educators) available in either the Mac or PC version at www.halfbakedsoftware.com/index.php, and create one lesson for the language you teach. Write a separate introduction to this CALL lesson that includes your learning objectives (i.e., discrete goals), the L2 language level, and how you will test students on the same material after completing your exercise. Share your CALL lesson with your colleagues and ask for comments.

4.   After doing activity 3, review the CALL lesson produced by a colleague/classmate and use the criteria of "learner fit" and "teacher fit."

5.   Write a review of some commercially available software that deals with the language you teach, following the CALICO guides (https://calico.org/p-21-SoftwareReviews.html - Courseware).

6.   Discuss the ultimate goals of L2 instruction. Is it possible to reach mastery of an L2 through classroom language instruction? Bley-Vroman (1990) and others would argue that it is not possible. Discuss whether their findings invalidate the goals of the language programs at the high school and university levels? Give reasons why not. What role does CALL play?

7.   Conduct a survey of your colleagues and students to determine how much feedback (i.e., error correction) and of what type they would like to have available in a CALL program. Discuss whether their requests are practical given today's state of technology and the cost of producing CALL programs.

NOTES

1. See http://unicode.org.
2. In the commercial realm, *Who Is Oscar Lake?* provided simulations similar to the Athena project that used a video game/mystery approach to CALL.
3. For CALICO Review, see https://calico.org/p - 21-SoftwareReviews.html Courseware; for FLTEACH, see www.cortland.edu/flteach/flteach-res.html.

4. See also www-ai.ijs.si/eliza/eliza.html.

5. See www.eurocall-languages.org/research/research_policy.html.

6. www.eurocall-languages.org/research/research policy.htm.

7. The MLA policy statement is found at www.mla.org/guidelines_evaluation _digital.

8. www.mla.org/guidelines evaluation digital.

9. See www.wordchamp.com/lingua2/Home.do.

10. As part of a CALL workshop, the Language Resource Center at San Diego State University offers a very thorough list of currently available authoring tools and test-making tools at http://balrog.sdsu.edu/~wstrombe/test_authoring_systems .htm.

11. For Yale's Center for Language Study Comet templates, see http://comet.cls.yale .edu/about/index.html. For CLEAR's SMILE templates, see http://clear.msu .edu/clear/store/products.php?product_category=online.

12. See www.halfbakedsoftware.com/index.php; http://hotpot.uvic.ca/index.htm.

13. See www-writing.berkeley.edu/chorus/call/cuttingedge.html.

14. Schulze (2001) is responding, in part, to Salaberry's (1996) criticisms of iCALL.

15. For E-Tutor, see www.e-tutor.org; for Robo-Sensei, see www.usfca.edu/ japanese/Rsdemo/preRSfiles/index.htm; for Tagarela, see http://tagarela.osu .edu.

16. See www.auralog.com/english.html.

17. Available from www.ict4lt.org/. See "Software and Website Evaluation Forms," www.ict4lt.org/en/index.htm.

18. See https://calico.org/p 21-SoftwareReviews.html – Courseware.

Chapter 4

Computer-Mediated
Communication (CMC)

BACKGROUND

From the brief survey of SLA theories presented in chapter 1, it should be clear that best practices in FL teaching need to be firmly grounded in interactionist notions of one flavor or another: for example, the proximal zone of development, negotiation of meaning, FonF, task-based learning, project-based learning, or pair collaboration. These constructs, simple or complex, rely on the power of human interactions to stimulate the process of SLA (O'Rourke 2005, 436–37). While cooperative exchanges—whether learner-learner or native speaker-learner (see Blake and Zyzik 2003)—cannot be said to be a direct cause of SLA, they most certainly get students ready to learn, as Gass (1997, 130) has explained, by focusing attention on unfamiliar structures (i.e., "noticing," in Schmidt's 1990 term) and by providing the necessary scaffolding in the learning environment (Bruner 1996).

Not surprisingly, talented classroom teachers actively seek to provide opportunities for their students to engage in collaborative interactions. Teachers can create the same opportunities for interactions within the context of *computer-mediated communication* (*CMC*), whether in real time (*synchronous, SCMC*) or deferred time (*asynchronous, ACMC*). Kern and Warschauer (2000) have labeled this communication in service of language learning as network-based language teaching (NBLT), which includes e-mail, discussion forums or electronic bulletin boards, blogs, wikis, and chatting with or without sound/video. The potential benefits of collaborative exchanges, whether set in the classroom or managed online, depend more on sound pedagogical design of the tasks the participants are asked to accomplish than on the actual locus of the learning event. In the rest of this chapter, both asynchronous and synchronous CMC tools will be reviewed, along with a close examination of the discourse that students produce when they engage in online communication.[1] Finally, the Cultura project developed at MIT will be showcased as an ideal way to use technology in service of developing *intercultural communicative competence* (*ICC*), the ultimate goal of L2 language study for all those in pursuit of becoming bilingual.

ASYNCHRONOUS CMC

Godwin-Jones (2003a, 12) makes a distinction between first- and second-generation tools for the Internet, the former being widely familiar to most Internet users and the latter being built on a new technology know as XMI. (extensible markup language), as opposed to HTML (see chapter 2).

First-generation CMC Tools

First-generation tools include e-mail, electronic mailing lists, and discussion forums, also known as threaded bulletin boards. Most e-mail clients (e.g., Outlook, Thunderbird, Eudora) now support formatted text (i.e., not just ASCII text), non-Roman fonts, and the capacity to attach photos, graphics, and even sound/video (see following review of Wimba). The same is true of web-based e-mail programs such as Microsoft's Hotmail, the only difference being that the web-based programs can be accessed directly using a web browser without downloading a separate client or special e-mail program. When all else fails, e-mail is the lowest common denominator for exchanging information and ideas with students from the same class or from around the world. E-mail is the default technology used by tandem learning, an organization that pairs two people who wish to learn each other's language and focuses in pedagogical terms on the principles of reciprocity and learner autonomy (O'Rourke 2005, 434).[2]

Despite new technological advances, e-mail has not lost any of its usefulness within the Internet landscape, especially as everyone is so willing to engage in e-mail exchanges and because this platform is supported with minimal access to the Internet either via the super highway (i.e., broadband, Internet II) or back alleys (i.e., 28K modem).

Electronic mailing lists (listservs) comprised of a group of e-mail users are another frequently used tool in both commerce and education. A message sent to a listserv goes out to everyone registered in the group. Many universities automatically provide their instructors with class listservs linked to their respective courses and student enrollments. Listserv participants need only remember that when wishing to respond to a single individual rather than the whole group, they must replace the general listserv address with the individual's unique e-mail address—otherwise, everyone in the group will read what might be a personal message. This error might seem obvious to the reader, but it is repeated on a daily basis, much to the embarrassment of some and the irritation of others from the listserv.

Teachers often use listservs to their advantage as the best medium for posting general class announcements because the ubiquitous medium of e-mail/listserv guarantees that everyone in the class will receive the pertinent information. While students do not always log on to a course management system, they almost always check their e-mail. But for most interactive exchanges, discussion forums or electronic bulletin boards are preferred.[3]

Discussion forums automatically maintain a record of all messages in a threaded or hierarchical structure. Each topic represents one thread that others in the forum can respond to. The instructor can determine who can begin new threads or topics: only instructors or everyone in the class. Forums, like listservs, are semipublic writing areas, as opposed to e-mail, which is a private and more informal CMC medium. Forums are a pervasive feature of course management systems such as WebCT, Blackboard, and Moodle and have been considered a cardinal tool for asynchronous distance learning for a long time (see chapter 5).

Wimba markets a variety of CMC tools, including a threaded discussion tool called Voice Board that allows users not only to exchange text messages under separate threads but also to add sound recordings (Blake 2005b).[4] At the heart of Wimba's tools lies an open source sound compression technology (Speex) and the respective applets, which are written in Java and capitalize on an advanced algorithm geared toward saving bandwidth while maintaining sound quality. The Wimba applets use HTTP as the communication medium and therefore are capable of passing through most firewalls and run under a

28K modem environment or better. Administrators and power users can choose the recording level quality from 8 kbit/s to 44 kbit/s, with the default norm for modem use being set at 12 kbit/s. There is no limit to the number of users. Voice Boards can be inserted into any web page with a few lines of JavaScript that invoke the Wimba applet and point to the server where the requested sounds are stored. Threads are displayed in standard tree-view fashion. Each thread indicates if there are other associated threads by means of a "+" or "−" sign. Clicking the + sign to the left of a top-level thread will expand it. Clicking any post will display the previously posted text along with sound controls to play the recorded sound at the bottom of the screen.

Voice Boards can be made "public." This means that users can then reply to any previous post or reply or return to the main board to compose a new thread with or without attached voice following the standard protocol used by any bulletin board. Alternately, instructors can disable the students' ability to compose new threads, giving them only the ability to respond to instructor-led, top-level threads. In addition, if a Voice Board is made "private," discussion is restricted between instructor and student. In this case, only instructors can post top-level threads, available to all students. Students then respond to instructors; only instructors and the individual who composed the reply can see this message. When an instructor responds, his or her message is only available to him or her and the student recipient of the message. In essence, private Voice Boards provide an easy and quick gateway to online assessments and testing, where instructors can post top-level questions and students are blocked from viewing one another's responses or teacher feedback. Whether using public or private boards, there is no limit to the number of threads or responses that can be added. In a similar fashion, Wimba allows voice attachments to e-mails as well.

Godwin-Jones (2003a) considers discussion forums as an equalizing tool where universal participation is encouraged as opposed to the more complicated dynamics found in face-to-face dialogues, where certain individuals can dominate the flow of the discourse. However, Payne (2004, 159) cautions that participating in asynchronous discussion forums is not the same as doing a writing assignment; rather, it's more like a protracted conversation that takes place over time. Teachers need to think about structuring interaction in online learning much more than in the classroom because online activities such as forums cannot be fine-tuned on the fly in the same way as discussions in the classroom context. Students carry out these activities by themselves on their own time, away from the eyes of the instructor. Clear instructions, goals, and learning objectives are imperative if the tasks are going to succeed.

Second-generation CMC Tools

Blogs and wikis are examples of second-generation asynchronous Internet tools. Blogs can be described as online hypertext journals that others read and react to. The reactions are logged and posted chronologically and become part of the blog. Most blogs are personal or journalistic in nature (Godwin-Jones 2003a; Ducate and Lomicka 2005) and, as such, allow students to exercise their own voice with a freedom that cannot be experienced in moderated discussion forums. By the same token, blogs demand more personal responsibility from students than forums, as only one student is ultimately responsible for publishing an online diary. Obviously, blogs also afford the student the possibility of reaching a public beyond the confines of the classroom through publishing a record of the student's thought. A blog requires no special knowledge of HTML; the interface offers a WYSIWYG editing palette where students can choose how they wish to format text or insert graphics or other multimedia objects.[5] Reynard (2007) maintains that blogs can be used effectively to develop each student's individual learning voice but only if they are intentionally designed into the course and are clearly valued throughout the course to ensure student motivation and participation. She contends that blogs used as a mere assignment add-on will have little reflection value for the student.

Wikis (*wiki* is Hawaiian for "quick") are similar to blogs but are a group product rather than the initiative of one individual. Wikis share the blog's WYSIWYG editing environment that makes adding to or modifying content extremely easy. Wikis, however, are not simply chronologically oriented but rather allow the group to reorganize content as they see fit. Any participant can add, modify, rearrange, or even destroy text, images, and other multimedia objects from earlier contributions. The wiki keeps a record of all modifications and allows any participant to regress to a previous content state. Any change or regression affects everyone working on the wiki. Consequently working together on a wiki has the potential to be counterproductive if the participants enter into constant revisionist war over content and form. Conversely, a wiki provides the ideal tool with which to carry out collaborative writing and project-based work. The goal of a wiki site is to become a shared repository of knowledge, with the knowledge base growing over time. Unlike chat rooms, wiki content is expected to have some degree of seriousness and permanence. For instance, Moodle allows users to create multiple wikis with full Unicode compliance. Students of Arabic, for instance, can work on their Arabic writing and ask each other questions, alternating between Arabic and English, through the wiki.

SYNCHRONOUS CMC (SCMC)

Early attempts at using SCMC programs for language teaching were carried out in chat rooms where large groups or even a whole class would log on and chat at once, usually from the same language lab. Daedalus Interchange was one of the first programs to be used in this way, especially by English composition teachers. Kern (1995) reported that L2 students of French using Daedalus wrote much more and produced more turns than students talking face-to-face in the classroom (an average of 12.5 versus 5.3 turns) but frequently with less linguistic accuracy than teachers would normally demand from a written medium such as a formal composition assignment. Similarly, Chun (1994) found that the use of chat rooms promoted increased morphological complexity for fourth-semester L2 students of German.

Gradually the profession has begun to recognize that writing in a chat room is different from writing a formal composition at home as an assignment. Chat room discourse consists of language that is much closer to oral discourse than to written (Sotillo 2000). Programs from the computer gaming world, such as *MUDs (multiuser dungeon/domain)* and *MOOs (MUD object oriented)*, have also been adapted to the needs of teaching foreign languages in this early adoption phase (Thorne and Payne 2005, 379).

SCMC with Voice/Video Tools

More recently, language teachers have begun to employ SCMC in pairs or small groups with the idea of fostering as much task-based interaction as possible, sometimes with the addition of voice tools as well. Lafford and Lafford (2005) have reviewed a number of text-based chat programs intended for small group use and classified them under the label of IM tools. IM tools consist of a client program that participants first download to their respective computers and then log on to a particular system: for example, ICQ, MSN Messenger, Yahoo! Messenger, AOL's Instant Messenger (AIM), PalTalk, and iVisit (for another review of these tools, see Cziko and Park 2003). In order for students in any given class to connect to other users, they must create a buddy list using either e-mail addresses, account numbers, or screen names. Learning management systems such as Blackboard, WebCT, or Moodle offer their own internal chat programs within a more controlled learning environment where all students are automatically enrolled in a chat room.

Written chat comes in two different modes: one in which written entries are posted by means of a carriage return (i.e., IRC-style chat) and the other in which participants share a text field and a single cursor placed in a field with immediate display-style chat that updates the window character by character. Each modality has its advantages and disadvantages. With the immediate display-style chat, participants can see the thought process of their partners evolving on the screen, but a protocol for who gets to write at any one time must be clearly worked out among participants. Otherwise, the chat partners could spend their time arguing over who has the stylus, with one person or the other endlessly rewriting previous contributions. The carriage-return modality allows anyone to post a message at any time, which empowers less assertive or inherently shy students. No one can stop someone else from posting ideas. Conversely, this modality produces long pauses while one's partner is typing. Frequently, questions go unanswered for several turns until the participants catch up with previous postings. This decalage, or lag effect, is disconcerting and even disruptive to the natural flow of any dialogue and takes some getting used to.

Payne (2004, 159) has identified the benefits of written SCMC:

- SCMC reduces the pace of discussion.
- Textual exchanges are posted and are therefore not ephemeral but rather ever present on the screen for students to consult and continue processing.

- Students have more time for linguistic processing to prepare their own contributions.
- Students' affective filters are lower in SCMC because no one is looking over their shoulder as is the case in face-to-face exchanges.

Wildner-Bassett (2005, 636–37) focuses, in particular, on CMC's spatial independence from the immediate face-to-face context to stress out-of-body experiences, a metaphor for increased opportunities for students engaging in CMC to step back and contemplate new identities and voices that move students beyond preestablished categories. She envisages using SCMC to establish a particular learning ecology where "learners cooperate in their ways of knowing and of being together by revealing their processes of naming and critically viewing their own identities" (646). Wildner-Bassett cautions, as I did earlier in this chapter in reference to assigning asynchronous CMC tasks, that conscious stewardship by the teacher is necessary for this critical social-constructivist viewpoint to emerge. Ultimately both teachers and students are charged with creating a classroom climate where all voices can be heard and all participants are willing to listen (654).

Other benefits of a more controversial nature include claims that SCMC levels hierarchical differences originating from ethnicity, age, gender, and shyness (Thorne 2003). But much depends on the tasks, teachers, and idiosyncratic characteristics of the students themselves. What is clear is that students like to chat, so by assigning CMC tasks teachers can harness more of the students' time outside of class for L2 learning. After all, chatting is an activity that students know how to do and do frequently on a daily basis.

Currently the SCMC tools mentioned earlier are evolving or have already evolved to include audio features—either half-duplex (i.e., walkie-talkie type sound exchanges) or full-duplex (*voice-over IP* [*VoIP*] or telephonic sound exchanges)—and sometimes even video capacity, which obviously requires access to more bandwidth, which eliminates users with only 28K modem connections. In addition to their Voice Boards, Wimba also offers a synchronous Voice Direct tool with half-duplex sound and text exchange, with an option for archiving the audio and text exchanges (i.e., Wimba converts and saves a Voice Direct session into a chronologically organized Voice Board using their same patented applet technology). This archiving feature is very attractive to researchers doing CMC studies or to teachers who wish to follow their students' chat progress closely. Macromedia also offers a synchronous CMC product called Breeze with similar features based on the infrastructure of a Flash communication server. With Breeze, students need only install a Flash plug-in with their favorite web browser—no separate client downloads are needed. The Flash plug-in approach is attractive because everyone has a favorite browser and computer configuration. Installing a single Flash plug-in, which most people need anyway to view web pages with animation or sophisticated graphics, represents an elegant solution. In addition to VoIP voice/video, Breeze allows users to employ both written modalities described earlier, carriage-return or immediate-display text entry.

Given their respective dependence on a robust server infrastructure, both Wimba and Breeze come with hefty price tags that require a substantial institutional commitment. The Skype client, conversely, is free when chatting from computer to computer with up to four people (Skype charges to connect to cell phones).[6] By setting up a SkypeCast, an unlimited number of people can join in a telephonic (VoIP) conversation.[7] The Skype algorithm yields surprisingly high audio quality over large distances with relatively short time delays (at most, one or two seconds). One drawback is the lack of any archiving features. However, Skype also offers a written chat mode that can be saved. As with all SCMC programs, buying an inexpensive set of earphones is well worth it to eliminate feedback loop effects.

A recent voice chat newcomer that also uses a Flash communication server is YackPack.com. Their Walkie Talkie widget can be inserted into any web, blog, or wiki to allow all users the ability to exchange telephonic voice on the fly (i.e., VoIP). When the user sets up a Walkie Talkie widget, YackPack provides the code for its instantiation that can be copied and inserted into any web page. As long as the other users also have the Flash plug-in installed, this tool—a product of B. J. Fogg's Persuasive Technology Lab at Stanford University (Fogg 2003)—works seamlessly with no additional setup or installation of a separate client.[8] YackPack is completely web-based and free.

In the interactionist literature, there are numerous studies that illustrate the benefits of face-to-face negotiations carried out between native and nonnative speakers (Lomicka 2006, 213). Students can enhance cultural awareness, motivate themselves to engage in real interactions, increase the quantity of their oral production, explore stereotypes, and establish a personal connection with the target language/culture. Similar benefits, including a heightened focus on form, have also been demonstrated for pairs engaging in SCMC (Blake 2000) and include native speakers chatting with nonnative speakers, NS/NNS; heritage speakers chatting with nonnative speakers, HS/NNS (Blake and Zyzik 2003); and nonnative speakers chatting with nonnative speakers, NNS/NNS. In the following sections I discuss the NNS/NNS context and describe the ideal conditions for its use, and I provide a case study of a bimodal SCMC tool that allows the exchange of both text and audio chat.

Intracultural CMC

Proponents of the interaction hypothesis (e.g., Gass 1997; Gass, Mackey, and Pica 1998; Long and Robinson 1998, among others) have established that face-to-face classroom negotiations play a fundamental role in SLA, although their results are highly sensitive to the type of tasks that the participants are asked to carry out (Pica, Kanagy, and Falodun 1993). Among the benefits cited, these negotiations tend to increase input comprehensibility through language modifications—such as simplifications, elaborations, confirmation and comprehension checks, clarifications requests, or recasts—which end up providing the L2 learner with the type of negative evidence deemed necessary by certain SLA theories for continued language development. This type of negotiation has also been described in the literature as focus on form (FonF), and is defined by Long (1991, 45–46): "Focus on form . . . overtly draws students' attention to linguistic elements as they arise incidentally in lessons whose overriding focus is on meaning or communication."

With respect to tasks, Pica, Kanagy, and Falodun (1993) classified tasks as either one-way or two-way exchanges, with the participants either reaching a single solution or not (± convergence). When working in dyads, jigsaw tasks provide each partner with only half the information needed to solve the communication task; the partners must share their respective parts equally (i.e., two-way task) and then try to converge on a single outcome. Information-gap tasks assume that only one person holds the pertinent information, which the other partner must solicit (i.e., this constitutes a one-way task, but the task can be repeated with the roles reversed in order to form a two-way task), whether or not a unique outcome is predictable. Pica, Kanagy, and Falodun predicted that jigsaw and information-gap tasks would promote more of these negotiations than other task stimuli. They also observed that negotiations took the discursive form of a trigger (the occurrence of a particular linguistic feature that causes a misunderstanding), an indicator (explicit notice that a misunderstanding has occurred), a response (an effort to repair the misunderstanding), and a reaction (an acknowledgment that the repair was successful). The benefits of negotiations of meaning were first demonstrated for learner-native speaker oral discussions (Hatch 1978; Holliday 1995; Long 1981), but further investigations registered the same benefits for learner-learner oral discussions as well (Varonis and Gass 1985; Gass and Varonis 1994).

Other researchers (Blake 2000, 2006; Pellettieri 2000; Sotillo 2000; Smith 2003) have documented how SCMC negotiations of meaning obtain similar benefits to those found in face-to-face exchanges, although Smith (2003) felt it necessary to add two additional functions—confirmations and reconfirmations—to the CMC discourse paradigm in order to compensate for the delayed nature of the communication that is endemic to the IRC-style chat.

Abrams (2006) has christened task-based learner-learner CMC as intracultural communication and attests to its wide use in college-level L2 classrooms. Both Blake (2000) and Smith (2003) claim that the majority of spontaneous negotiations in online intracultural communication deal with lexical confusions or misunderstandings. However, Pellettieri (2000) reports that carefully designed tasks can yield similar benefits for morphological and syntactic topics as well. Sotillo's (2000, 470–71) study of written CMC discourse showed that whereas written SCMC was similar to face-to-face communication in terms of discourse functions and syntactic complexity, ACMC writing promoted more sustained interactions and greater syntactic complexity.

Doughty and Long (2003b) have approached SCMC with the aim of establishing the most propitious psycholinguistic environment for its implementation. They provide ten methodological principles (MPs) or language teacher universals that instructors should follow when implementing SCMC tasks, with an eye to stimulating negotiations and L2 language development.

- Use tasks, not texts, as the unit of analysis; it's the process that makes the difference in SLA.
- Promote learning by doing.
- Elaborate input through negotiations of meaning (do not simplify the linguistic material; do not rely solely on authentic texts).

- Provide rich (not impoverished) input in terms of quality, quantity, variety, genuineness, and relevance.
- Encourage inductive ("chunk") learning through implicit instruction.
- Focus on form through meaning-focused tasks that allow L2 students to notice their linguistic gaps (via input flooding, input elaboration, input enhancement, corrective feedback on errors, or input processing).
- Provide negative feedback (e.g., recasts) in order to induce noticing.
- Respect "learner syllabuses"/developmental processes by providing input that is attuned to the learner's current processing capabilities.
- Promote cooperative/collaborative learning.
- Individualize instruction (according to communicative and psycholinguistic needs).

Many of Doughty and Long's MPs are intuitively applicable to the SCMC or ACMC context. In the following SCMC exchange between a Spanish instructor and a first-year learner, the reader will recognize the instructor's attempts to follow some of these MPs by elaborating input, providing rich input, supplying negative feedback for errors, using implicit instruction, stimulating collaborative learning, and individualizing the instruction to fit the learner's need at any particular moment. The teacher also uses sound and text to carry out the lesson plan, but applying these principles is not always as easy as it sounds. Sometimes an instructor misses the target. Fortunately, students are most forgiving of this in an SCMC collaborative environment because of an overarching concern to communicate effectively in L2.

Case Study of Bimodal SCMC

To date, few researchers have tried to analyze bimodal SCMC, or chatting that includes the capacity to exchange both text and audio messages (Blake 2005a). The SCMC examples examined here come from a regularly scheduled virtual office hour that an instructor of Spanish hosts every week with first-year students enrolled in a distance learning introductory Spanish class. The chat tool is home grown but relies on a Flash communication server, just like the commercially available product Breeze. This particular conversation between one adult student of beginning Spanish and her NS instructor represents the ideal SCMC situation of pair work. The potential for discursive confusions and management problems naturally escalates in direct proportion to the number of participants involved in a chat session.

Understandably, any protracted silences in a bimodal chat environment are routinely interpreted as signs that the other party failed to hear the previous utterance. In fact, the partner's silence might be due to thinking, slow typing, or utter confusion caused by the original question or some unknown linguistic form. In face-to-face conversation, these potential sources of breakdowns are mitigated by body language and phatic communication (e.g., "ok . . . right . . . ," "let's see . . . ," "right," "like . . . uh-huh . . . ," "oh . . . ," "ah . . . ," "you don't say"). This time-lag effect is unavoidable in the IRC-style chat and often prompts participants to resort to using the voice channel, if available, to establish some phatic contact, much like the cell phone advertisement where the salesman runs around everywhere saying, "Can you hear me now?"

The examples discussed later come from a first-year Spanish L2 student of low verbal ability, as judged by the instructor. Adjusting for different levels of proficiency, this student is representative of the types of exchanges that are possible with bimodal chatting, a technique that is not as easy to use as one initially might think. Both students and instructors can freely use both channels (i.e., sound and text) separately or more or less in tandem. It takes instructors a while to get used to using the textual mode as a support or backup to what students are practicing in the voice channel. For the instructor, it's a bit like using the blackboard in the classroom to record what's being said or to offer other pertinent information without interrupting the flow of sound conversation.

With respect to the transcripts, the time stamp is provided at the end of each exchange to document the flow of the conversation and the alternations between the text and voice modalities. Sound exchanges are all in capital letters, and code-switching between languages is shown in italics. Certain portions of the text are highlighted in bold to draw attention to a particular grammatical or discursive point under question.

Notice in (1) how the instructor insists that the student practice orally as well as textually so that the instructor is able to evaluate the student's responses for pronunciation and syntactic accuracy. In this fashion, the instructor can then provide the appropriate feedback with both oral and textual reinforcements and hints. The instructor also indulges in frequent repetitions and recasts of a highly didactic nature, much like the discourse often heard within the walls of a typical language classroom. Lee (2004) has described this type of exchange as linguistic scaffolding on the part of the more experienced partner. As discussed earlier, the instructor interprets the student's slowness to respond as a sign that she didn't previously hear the instructor's helpful responses. The truth is that the student heard them but didn't understand, causing a complete breakdown in the conversation and the need for negotiation or repair in order to get the exchange flowing again.

(1) MAKING STUDENTS PRACTICE
VIA THE ORAL CHANNEL

STUDENT:	Que "trajajaste"? 20:37:19 [What [is] *trabajaste?*]
INSTRUCTOR:	Did you work? 20:37:26
INSTRUCTOR:	YA ESTOY AQUÍ CON MICROFONO. YA HE ARREGLADO EL PROBLEMA. EH . . . ¿**TRABAJASTE** HOY EN TU ESPANOL, NANCY? 20:37:40 [I'm here with the microphone. I've solved the problem. Did you work today on your Spanish?]
STUDENT:	¿OTRA VEZ? 20:37:44 [Again?]
INSTRUCTOR:	¿ME PUEDES OIR? 20:38:3 [Can you hear me?]
STUDENT:	**Trabajaste**? 20:38:08 [*Trabajaste?* [What's that mean?]]
INSTRUCTOR:	¿Me escuchas? 20:38:12 [Can you hear me?]
INSTRUCTOR:	SI ¿TRABAJASTE? *DID YOU WORK?* ¿TRABAJASTE? SÍ, TRABAJÉ. 20:38:18 [Yes, did you work? *Did you work?* Did you work? Yes, I worked.]
STUDENT:	No comprendo. 20:38:25 [I don't understand.]
INSTRUCTOR:	Háblame por favor. 20:38:34. [Please talk to me.]

As a follow-up comment on (1), note that the instructor's introduction of a verb in the preterit, an unfamiliar tense at this point in a first-year course, precipitates the breakdown here. The same would be true for the classroom environment: new grammatical material causes a disruption in the communicative flow of the discourse that can only be resolved through intense efforts to negotiate the meaning of the past tense. The instructor uses the voice channel in order to model what the student should reply to the original question: "Did you work?" But the student is totally confused by this new verb form and falls silent. Then she wonders if *trabajé* ('I worked') is a third-person form in the present tense. The instructor finally realizes her misstep, as shown in (2); the negotiations process has made apparent to both individuals the root of the problem:

(2) BREAKDOWN, NEGOTIATION, AND REPAIR

STUDENT: That is the entire question? 20:38:48

INSTRUCTOR: ¿A QUÉ TE REFIERES? *THAT'S THE ENTIRE QUESTION.* ¿QUÉ PREGUNTAS? ¿TRABAJASTE? SI. TRABAJÉ, TRABAJÉ EN MI ESPAÑOL. 20:38:59 [What are you referring to? *That's the entire question.* What are you asking? Did you work? Yes, I worked. I worked on my Spanish.]

INSTRUCTOR: ¿PUEDES REPETIR, NANCY? 20:39:21 [Could you repeat, Nancy?]

STUDENT: **Trabajé is third person word.** 20:39:35

STUDENT: Pero trabajaste? 20:39:52 [But what about *trabajaste*?]

INSTRUCTOR: No, trabajé es la primera persona pero es pasado. 20:39:53 [No, *trabajé* is the first person but it's the past.]

INSTRUCTOR: EH . . . NANCY, NO. TRABAJÉ ES PRIMERA PERSONA. PERO ES PASADO. *YOU DIDN'T STUDY PASADO YET.* ¿DE ACUERDO? 20:39:57 [Nancy, no. *Trabajé* is first person but it's the past. You didn't [*sic*] study past yet. Ok?]

As in face-to-face interactions, one of the most important benefits of SCMC chat centers around what Swain (2000) has called forced output. For Swain, forced output means that students monitor their own interlanguage much more closely precisely because they must use L2 syntax to formulate their responses—they have no other choice. The results from this type of output create a feedback loop that creates new input for the learner and a second chance to get it right—in other words, forced output feeds self-correction and, in time, structural integration, as can be seen in oral exchanges in (3). Not only does this L2 student finally retrieve the correct word in Spanish for *since*, but also she corrects her first incorrect attempt at translating "in the afternoon (P.M.)," which was based on an English calque. The final sound transmission gets it all correct, undoubtedly, to the student's great sense of personal satisfaction.

(3) SELF-CORRECTION AS A RESULT OF FORCED OUTPUT

STUDENT: ¿PROFESORA? ¿DÓNDE ESTÁ CINDY? 20:24:45 [Professor? Where is Cindy?]

INSTRUCTOR: NO SE, NO SÉ DONDE ESTÁ. ¿TÚ ESTÁS ALLÍ DESDE LAS OCHO? 20:24:5 [I don't know; I don't know where she is. You've been there since eight?]

INSTRUCTOR: TÚ TE CONECTASTE A LAS OCHO Y CINDY NO ESTABA, ¿CIERTO? 20:24:9 [You connected at eight and Cindy wasn't there, right?]

INSTRUCTOR: PERFECTO, NANCY, PERFECTO. TENEMOS OTRO ESTUDIANTE QUE SE LLAMA "ED" PERO NO ESTÁ TAMPOCO. NO SE, A LO MEJOR TIENE PROBLEMAS CON LA CONEXIÓN, ¿COMPREN-DES? 20:25:11 [Perfect, Nancy, perfect. We have another student named Ed but he's not online either. I don't know . . . maybe he has connection problems, do you understand?]

STUDENT: Uh . . . TENGO . . . UH . . . TENGO . . . UH. LO . . . (NO, THAT'S WRONG), TENGO . . . OCHO EN TARDE. 20:25:32 [Uh, I have, uh, I have, uh, the . . . (No, that's wrong), I have . . . eight in evening.]

STUDENT: LO SIENTO. NO COMPRENDO. 20:25:8 [I'm sorry. I don't understand.]

INSTRUCTOR: ¿TRABAJASTE CON EL? 20:25:53 [Do you work with him?]

STUDENT: NO CINDY *SINCE* OCHO EN TARDE. 20:26:28 [No Cindy *since* eight in evening.]

STUDENT:	DESDE ... NO CINDY **DESDE LAS OCHO EN TARDE ... DE LA TARDE.** 20:26:42 [Since ... no Cindy ... since eight in evening ... in the evening.]
STUDENT:	NO CINDY DESDE LAS OCHO DE LA TARDE. 20:26:58 [No Cindy [has been here] since eight in the evening.]

Another advantage often associated with chatting stems from the ease with which students can direct their own linguistic progress. As in (4), the student can stop the flow of conversation with the instructor at any time, demand immediate answers to linguistic problems or miscommunications, and subsequently try out new responses for accuracy. This particular student has had little experience with the common verbal expression *to like* (*gustar*), which in Spanish behaves syntactically as an unaccusative verb where the logical object becomes the surface subject (i.e., "It pleases [likes] me ..."). In experimenting with *gustar* the student gets in over her head and uses a superlative adverb incorrectly—or so it appears. The instructor corrects her, but that is not what the student had in mind; the student quickly asks for a translation of the adverbial expression *too much*. The student chooses to use only the written chat interface, as opposed to the voice channel, because it gives her more of an equal footing with the instructor to direct the path of conversation and to solve her own communication difficulties.

(4) STUDENT-DIRECTED LEARNING AND ERROR CORRECTION

STUDENT:	Voy a escribir. 20:45:21 [I'm going to write.]
INSTRUCTOR:	Dime (tell me). ¿Qué te gusta comer? 20:45:42. [Tell me. What do you like to eat?]
INSTRUCTOR:	A mí me gusta comer patatas fritas y huevo. ¿y a ti? 20:46:10 [Me, I like to eat french fries and eggs. And you?]
INSTRUCTOR:	What do you like to eat? 20:46:21
STUDENT:	Es ortro tiempo? 20:46:23 [Is that another tense?]
INSTRUCTOR:	Es presente. 20:46:34 [It's the present tense.]

INSTRUCTOR:	Pero es la expresión de gustar. **Me gusta, te gusta, le gusta** . . . 20:46:58 [But it's the expression *GUSTAR*. I like, you like, s/he likes.]
STUDENT:	Me gusta spaghetti y italiano. 20:47:29 [I like spaghetti and Italian.]
STUDENT:	Me gusta chocolate. 20:47:41 [I like chocolate.]
STUDENT:	**Me gusta muy mucho.** 20:47:54 [I like it muchly much.]
INSTRUCTOR:	Me gusta muchísimo. **Es incorrecto decir [muy mucho]** 20:48:19 [I like it very much. It's incorrect to say "muchly much."]
INSTRUCTOR:	¿Te gusta comer espaguetis? 20:48:38 [Do you like to eat spaghetti?]
STUDENT:	How do you say "too much"? 20:48:44 [How do you say "too much"?]
INSTRUCTOR:	demasiado. 20:48:55.140316 [too much]
STUDENT:	Me gusta demasiado. 20:49:16 [I like it too much.]
INSTRUCTOR:	How do you say: Cómo se dice. 20:49:25.
STUDENT:	No . . **Me gusta comir damasiado.** 20:49:35 [No . . . I like to eat too much.]
STUDENT:	Como se dice? 20:49:49 [How do you say?]
STUDENT:	Sí. 20:49:54 [Yes.]

Despite the student's initial success with *gustar*, the real syntactic difficulty for the L2 learner revolves around choosing the correct indirect object that signals who experiences this sensation of pleasure (i.e., liking). An additional complication arises from the requirement to make *gustar* agree with what is the surface subject, but in reality is the semantic object or theme noun: for example, "*Me gusta eso*" (That likes me). To complicate matters more, the indirect object clitic is often accompanied by a full co-referential NP introduced by the personal *a*: "*A mi esposo le gusta la carne*" (My husband, he likes meat).[9] The instructor successfully leads the student to grasp this last point by offering the student a series of recasts that model the proper response, but as she tries to echo what the instructor has provided as a model, she neglects to change the narrative point of view. For example, the instructor says "Do you like it?" and the student replies incorrectly "Yes, **you** like it," instead of "**I** like it."

The instructor ignores the relatively minor spelling mistakes and uses a textual response to resolve these misunderstandings, much to the student's relief (e.g., Whew 21:02:41). In general, faulty spelling is less problematic in written chat than faulty pronunciation is for face-to-face negotiations or voice chat exchanges (O'Rourke 2005, 459).

(5) NOTICING THE GAP

STUDENT:	Mi esposo te gusta patatas fritas. 20:55:59 [My husband, you like french fries (←My husband, french fries is pleasing to you).]
INSTRUCTOR:	A mí esposo le gustan las patatas fritas. 20:56:16 [My husband, he likeS french fries.]
STUDENT:	Y carne. 20:56:29 [And meat.]
INSTRUCTOR:	Ah! Tu esposo no es vegetariano, ¿verdad? 20:56:43 [Ah, your husband isn't a vegetarian, right?]
STUDENT:	Mi esposo le gustan las patatas fritas y carne. 20:56:51 [My husband, he likes french fries and meat.]
STUDENT:	No es vegetariano. 20:57:08 [He's not a vegetarian.]
INSTRUCTOR:	A mí esposo también le gusta la carne y las patatas fritas. 20:57:16 [My husband, he also likes meat and french fries.]
INSTRUCTOR:	¿Tú eres vegetariana? 20:57:27 [Are you a vegetarian?]
STUDENT:	No, pero ensaldas y frutas. 20:57:47 [No, but salads and fruits.]
INSTRUCTOR:	No, pero te gusta comer ensaladas y frutas. 20:58:03 [No, but you like to eat salads and fruits.]
STUDENT:	No, pero te gusta comer ensaladas y frutas. 20:58:15 [No, but you like to eat salads and fruits.]
INSTRUCTOR:	A mí también me gusta comer ensaladas y frutas. 20:58:28 [Me, I also like to eat salads and fruits.]
INSTRUCTOR:	*me,* **when you talk about you as I like;** *te,* **when you talk about you, you like.** 20:59:24 [I (when you . . .) YOU (when you . . .).]
INSTRUCTOR:	Otra vez. 20:59:36 [Come again?]
INSTRUCTOR:	Qué TE gusta comer? 20:59:48 [What do YOU like to eat?]
INSTRUCTOR:	Otra vez (again). 21:00:01 [Again?]
STUDENT:	Me gusta comer ensaladas y frutas. 21:00:25 [I like to eat salads and fruits.]

STUDENT:	Correcto? 21:00:47. [Is that correct?]
INSTRUCTOR:	Sí, es correcto. Y a tu esposo, ¿Qué le gusta comer a él? 21:00:58 [Yes, that's correct. And your husband, what does he like to eat?]
STUDENT:	A mi esposo te gusta comer patatas fritas y carne. 21:01:37 [My husband, you like to eat french fries and meat.]
STUDENT:	Corrector? 21:01:50 [Correct?]
STUDENT:	Correcto? 21:01:55 [Correct?]
STUDENT:	Lo siento. 21:02:01 [Sorry (for the misspelling).]
INSTRUCTOR:	No. A mi esposo **le gusta**. 21:02:04 [No. My husband, he likes.]
STUDENT:	A mi esposa le guasta comer patatas fritas y carne. 21:02:25 [My husband, he likes to eat french fries and meat.]
STUDENT:	gusta. 21:02:30 [likes.]
INSTRUCTOR:	Ahora sí. 21:02:33 [Now it's correct.]
STUDENT:	Whew. 21:02:41

The true test of success, however, comes when the instructor shifts the focus to a different third party, Michelle, the student's daughter. By now the student has had sufficient written practice in producing *gustar*-type constructions so that changing the reference to the new person presents few problems, as seen in (6); only the personal *a* is still missing, but that error is extremely common with L2 students right up into the third year of Spanish language study (Montrul 2004). At such a time when the student finally drops the redundant *a Michelle* altogether or puts it after the verb (rather than following the typical English SVO syntactic pattern), a more proficient level of language competence will have been achieved.

(6) EXPLICIT CORRECTION AND PRACTICE MAKES PERFECT

INSTRUCTOR:	Qué le gusta a tu hija Michelle? 21:02:49 [What does your daughter Michelle like?]

STUDENT: Michelle le gusta comer ensalads y margaritas.
21:03:13 [Michelle, she likes to eat salads and margaritas.]

Notice from the examples in (5) and (6) that both the student and instructor depend heavily on textual clues to raise the student's metalinguistic
awareness. But do these explicit discussions transfer into acceptable oral
production as well? At the right moment in the exchange, the instructor
switches to the sound mode and peppers the student with a series of oral
questions until the student finally responds in kind—the final test of
whether the *gustar* construction is beginning to sink in. Both the written
production and the oral utterance of "*A mi gato le gusta comer...*"
(21:07:20) constitutes convincing evidence that the student is gaining considerable control over this new syntactic structure.

(7) SWITCHING INTO "OVERDRIVE"—THE ORAL MODE

INSTRUCTOR: Y a tu gato? 21:04:43 [And your cat?]

INSTRUCTOR: NANCY, ¿QUE LE GUSTA COMER A TU GATO?
21:05:12 [Nancy, what does your cat like to eat?]

STUDENT: A mi gato le gusta comer (too much)? 21:05:55 [My
cat, he likes to eat (too much).]

STUDENT: desmaisdos? 21:06:16 [Too much?]

INSTRUCTOR: NANCY, ¿QUE TE GUSTA A TI COMER? ¿QUE TE
GUSTA? 21:06:34 [Nancy, what do you like to eat?
What do you like?]

INSTRUCTOR: **DEMASIADO. TOO MUCH IS DEMASIADO.**
21:06:40 [Too much. *Too much* is *demasiado*.]

STUDENT: A MI GATO LE GUSTA COMER *AND I WAS LOOK-
ING FOR THE WORD "TOO MUCH" BUT I CAN'T
FIND IT.* 21:07:20 [My cat, he likes to eat and I was
looking for the word "too much" but I can't find it.]

INSTRUCTOR: ¿QUE TE GUSTA COMER? ¿A MI? A MI ME GUSTA
COMER PATATAS FRITAS. ME GUSTA COMER
PATATAS FRITAS. Y A TI, ¿QUE TE GUSTA? 21:07:22
[What do you like to eat? Me? Me, I like to eat french

fries. Me, I like to eat french fries. And you, what do you like (to eat)?]

Despite the time/turn lag so typical of networked exchanges, the student finally responds to the teacher's more personalized question, "What do YOU like to eat?" (21:6:34), in an appropriate way, setting aside for the moment ungrammatical use of a noun in subject position unaccompanied by an article (e.g., *ensalada* [salad] without the article, instead of *la ensalada*): "A MI ME GUSTA ENSALADA." (21:9:36) [Me, I like salad].

What should be obvious from the analysis of these networked exchanges is that they parallel very closely how people carry out their face-to-face interactions and provide evidence for the small but steady steps forward in the SLA process, with allowances being made for the typical time lags that result from overlapping or delayed turn-taking in written SCMC. In fact, except for this delay effect, it would be difficult to distinguish the language and discourse routines displayed in (1) through (7) from other transcriptions derived from face-to-face learner/instructor talk taking place in the classroom. The sound channel for these SCMC exchanges plays an important role in providing confirmations that give both students and teachers a sense of accomplishment and successful collaboration.

Weekly sessions such as the one examined in (1) through (7) provide L2 students with the opportunity to bring alive the language they are studying either in the classroom or in the distance learning format (see chapter 5). Despite the highly entertaining nature of multimedia materials delivered via the web, nothing can replace human interaction. Online students need the give-and-take that occurs in SCMC exchanges in order to try out new hypotheses and receive immediate feedback, even if that feedback comes from other, less expert L2 learners (i.e., intracultural CMC). Ironically, with rising enrollment pressures, CMC exchanges such as those examined earlier might give the student more opportunities to interact than can normally be supported in face-to-face conversations due to crowded classrooms.

What the interactionist model does not overtly stress, however, is the learning of culture and the notion of *intercultural communicative competence* (*ICC*), a corollary of Hyme's concept of communicative competence. Sociocultural theory (Lantolf 2000) addresses the issue of L2 students' learning ICC and is the focus of the next section.

INTERCULTURAL CMC: TELECOLLABORATIONS

Another group of sociocultural researchers (Byram 1997; Belz 2002, 2003; Belz and Thorne 2006; Thorne 2003; O'Dowd 2003, 2005, and 2006; Lomicka 2006; Kern, Ware, and Warschauer 2004; Warschauer 2004) disfavor the purely interactionist SCMC paradigm outlined earlier because CMC is portrayed only from the standpoint of a particular tradition of information-processing that separates the environment from its users. For sociocultural theorists, negotiation of meaning is often reduced in the classroom to nothing more than getting students to manage transactions that are devoid of real L2 cultural import. The implicit assumption they reject is that transactional routines are somehow culture free, the same the world over, which is patently false.

Sociocultural researchers contrast intracultural CMC with intercultural CMC or intercultural communication for foreign language learning (ICFLL); (Thorne and Payne 2005a) to "draw attention to the complex nature of humans as sociocultural actors and technological setting as artifact and as mediators, rather than determiners of action and interaction" (O'Rourke 2005, 435). These ideas draw heavily on Byram (1997), who defines intercultural competence as "an ability to evaluate, critically and on the basis of explicit criteria, perspectives, practices and products in one's own and other cultures and countries" (Byram, Gribkova, and Starkey 2002, 9). In other words, the goals of the L2 student should be to become flexible and open to other cultures and ideas so as to be able to change one's own values and attitudes as a function of contact with the world. In essence, then, the L2 learner should be viewed as an emerging bilingual, someone who uses both L1 and L2, no matter how limited, to evaluate new experiences with the world. Kramsch (1993, 2000) describes this process in terms of the L2 learner trying to find a psychological third place somewhere between the native-like mindset of L1 and the evolving sense L2 language and culture.

With respect to a working definition of ICC, Lomicka (2006, 213) very astutely recognizes the commonality among (a) Kramsch's (1993, 2000) notion of the L2 learner's locating himself in a third place somewhere between native-like competence in L1 and the target language, (b) Byram's call for critical cultural awareness, and (c) Freinet (1994) and Cummins and Sayers's (1995) "recul," or distancing, that must take place as the L2 learner moves toward any meaningful kind of bilingualism. To be sure, the conceptualization of the target culture in a sociocultural framework has little to do with the idea of transferring "one complete 'essence' or 'reality' about the target culture" (O'Dowd 2006, 18), if that could ever be said to exist with either high culture or popular culture. For the sociocultural theorist, ICC deals with a more interactive and dialogic process taking place among the learner, the home culture, and the target culture.

The intercultural approach to CMC has also been called telecollaboration (Warschauer 1997b; Belz 2002). O'Dowd and Ritter (2006, 623) describe telecollaboration as "online communication used to bring together language learners in different countries in order to carry out collaborative projects or undertake intercultural exchanges." As such, telecollaboration is not a necessary feature of a distance learning language course but rather a component that can be added to any language course taught at a distance or not. O'Rourke (2005, 434) envisages telecollaboration as a socially and culturally situated activity engaged in by learners as agents who coconstruct not only shared meanings but also their own roles. In chapter 3 I employed the term *agency* in reference to Kern and Warschauer's (2000) description of the current stage of CALL development. This new research paradigm explicitly endorses a shift in pedagogical concerns to view the student as an actor who directly shapes and reshapes his or her universe.

One welcome result of this paradigmatic shift has been a heightened emphasis on intercultural pragmatics, an area mostly ignored in the FL curriculum but that often lies at the heart of so many communicative breakdowns for the L2 learner. Many of the sociocultural CMC studies report on the frequent and serious communicative breakdowns that occur when teachers fail to alert their students to the intercultural differences (see Cohen and Sykes 2006 for CALL lessons on Spanish pragmatics).

Lomicka (2006, 218) and Thorne and Payne (2005, 376) correctly point out that current ideas about ICC have their beginnings in Freinet's movement in France in the 1920s to establish intercultural learning networks, work that continues even today.[10] Cummins and Sayers (1995) adapted Freinet's model to the computer world by using e-mail as the medium of intercultural exchange. *Tandem language learning*, an arrangement where two native speakers of different languages communicate regularly with one another, each with the purpose of learning the other's language, is almost aimed at creating networks (O'Rourke 2005, 434), although ICC has not been particularly highlighted by its proponents (O'Rourke and Schwienhorst 2003).

How do teachers implement an effective ICC experience via CMC, especially in light of the well-documented failures that have occurred? The Cultura project offers teachers a highly structured curriculum designed to foster an intercultural learning network using CMC tools. In the following sections I showcase Cultura as one of the ideal ways to move students toward a new sense of ICC.

THE CULTURA PROJECT: INTERCULTURAL LEARNING AT ITS BEST

The Cultura project was developed at MIT in the late 1990s to allow L2 learners from two different cultures to improve their ICC and their linguistic base (Furstenberg et al. 2001; Levet and Waryn 2006; Bauer et al. 2006).[11] Students of the two respective countries (N.B.: the authors started with France and the United States) complete online questionnaires related to their cultural values and associations. These questionnaires can be based on word associations (e.g., What words do you associate with the word *freedom*?), sentence completions (e.g., A good citizen is someone who . . .), or reactions to situations (e.g., You see a mother hitting her child in the supermarket. How do you feel?). Other key topics include work, leisure, nature, race, gender, family, identity, education, government, citizenship, politeness, authority, and individualism.

Each group fills out the questionnaire in their native language so as to be able to express themselves fully. The results from both sets of students are then compiled and presented online. In addition to the questionnaires, learners are also supplied with online resources such as opinion polls and press articles from the two cultures that can support them in their investigation and understanding of their partner class's responses. Responses from previous classes are also archived online for further research and consultation. The respective teachers then guide their students in class to analyze the two lists side-by-side in order to find differences and similarities between the two groups' responses and identify the implied values, with the goal of showing students that "understanding the other culture requires more than a list" and "is grounded in developing a curiosity toward the culture of *otherness*" (Furstenberg et al. 2001). The challenge of the Cultura project is to make the L2 cultural values visible, accessible, and understandable. In the process, linguistic difficulties are analyzed, and grammar is introduced as needed.

Following this analysis, students from both countries meet in ACMC sessions to discuss their findings, pose queries, request clarification from their counterparts, analyze the semantic networks implicit in the questionnaire material, and begin to develop a better understanding of their respective cultural differences by delving into the cultural assumptions that lie beneath stated beliefs. In other words, both sets of students have to step back and reflect on their own cultural values and those of others. So begins the dynamic and never-ending process of students' finding their own third place. Afterward both groups of students continue to deepen their new insights by studying films, newspaper articles, and selected texts from anthropology, history, literature, or philosophy that deal with cross-cultural perspectives. Video conferences and/or SCMC sessions can be optionally added as well to heighten motivation and increase the personal relationships between the groups, if logistics are favorable (i.e., time differences and available equipment).

Finally students present their ideas and analyses orally in class using L2, continue discussing, and then turn in a series of written compositions dealing with their respective and collective observations. They also post the final observations in L1 online, which become fodder for further discussion between the two groups. Furstenberg et al. (2001, 79) describe the process: "Students are therefore listening and reading mostly in the target language, although not exclusively, as we will see later. Speech and writing are produced in both languages. The interaction between a 'foreign' language and a 'mother tongue' leads to an effective integration of conceptual differences." Hence the first step in the process of cultural literacy comes about through this constant interaction between languages.

This *Cultura* guide states that although the model is very flexible, there are five fundamental principles for this method:

- The students from the two schools involved should be similar in age and life experiences.
- Students should use L2 during class time and to write their essays but L1 to complete the questionnaires and the discussion forums.

- The discussion forums should always be asynchronous in order to nurture reflection and analysis.
- Cultura needs to be completely integrated into the classroom curriculum (or students won't take the work seriously).
- The project needs to take place over a long period of time, a minimum of eight weeks.

Furstenberg et al. (2001, 75) summarize their goals as follows: "Results from the Cultura experiment suggest that there is a significant structural difference between French and American semantic networks pertaining to the cultural items our students explored. Explicating these differences is one way to develop cultural literacy. This form of cultural literacy is not so much acquiring a checklist of 'knowledge,' as developing awareness of the relation between selfhood and otherness. Not only the target culture comes under study but fundamental elements that structure the source culture are revealed as well."

O'Dowd (2005, 47–51) takes issue with the stipulation that all the ACMC must be carried out in L1. In carrying out a Cultura exchange between Spanish and American students, he and the other American instructors compromised so that all students wrote about certain topics exclusively in English, about others only in Spanish, and about still others using the respective L1 according to the Cultura guidelines. This adjustment was necessitated by the Spaniards' lack of online access at their university and/or living environments and their need to practice English before their final exams.

Ironically, the role of the teacher is not lessened by the Cultura project; the dynamics call for more of an expert guide than the typical showman found in the teacher-centered classroom. The teacher is critical in giving students stimulating supporting materials, focusing on particular linguistic expressions, and generally knowing how to channel their students' reactions into constructive analytical patterns rather than emotional meltdowns or hasty generalizations that only serve to reinforce cultural stereotypes. On the micro level, the teacher draws attention to contradictions, irony, humor, and sarcasm in search of charged linguistic expressions that are the product of deeply ingrained values. This process does not necessarily lead either teachers or students to closure but rather to a persistent interrogatory approach to L2 culture. The teacher should insist that students provide evidence for their observations by quoting pertinent language or examples gleaned from the questionnaire, films, articles, or supplementary materials.

O'Dowd (2006, 139) finds the opposition between teacher-centered and student-centered NBLT to be too simplistic; more specifically, he rejects the portrait of the NBLT teacher as a "guide on the side" (O'Dowd 2003, 138). The cultural differences often present L2 students with an insurmountable barrier that only the teacher can remove using direct intervention. "Teachers need to lead classroom discussions, but they also need to explicitly develop learners' knowledge and skills and cultural awareness by providing factual information, by modeling the analysis of texts from the partner class, by helping learners to create their own correspondence and also by encouraging them to focus on the meanings which the target culture attributes to behavior as opposed to simply focusing on the behaviour itself. These, I would argue, are all teacher-centred or teacher-led activities which have a justifiable presence in the network-based foreign language classroom" (38).

Clearly L2 students, in addition to their respective linguistic limitations, are not naturally aware of how to carry out intercultural exchanges. Accordingly, no matter how the debate is framed, the findings in this study have highlighted the need for a proactive approach to telecollaboration and the necessity for teachers to play a constant role in organizing and adapting their guidelines and activities according to the circumstances with which they and their partner-teacher are confronted. Very often it will be this flexibility and willingness to react creatively to problems that will mean the difference between success and failure in online collaborations.

CMC AND BEST PRACTICE

The interactionist framework and the sociocultural approach may not be as much at odds as one might think. It is not coincidental that most telecollaboration projects and ICC activities involve intermediate or advanced L2 students. First-year students would be hard-pressed to successfully carry out deep intercultural reflections, such as that described earlier, using L2 as the basis of communication in either a classroom or a CMC context.

When one thinks about face-to-face interaction or CMC, it is hoped that students are negotiating meaning, noticing gaps, working collaboratively, and directing the discourse in ways that satisfy their own particular learning concerns of the moment. As students gain more L2 competence, the opportunities to reflect on and absorb new cultural values must expand accordingly. Intermediate and advanced students cannot remain stunted in a never-ending transactional universe; they need to tackle the ever demanding and constantly shifting challenge of developing real ICC on their road to bilingualism.

The classroom reality, at all levels, is often very different, especially as many FL classrooms continue to endorse teacher-centered rather than more student-centered approaches. At the beginning levels, the asymmetric power relationship between the teacher, the all-knowing expert, and the L2 beginner can pose a significant deterrent to fostering the necessary interactions that prime the SLA pump, over and beyond the usual affective barriers engendered by worry over public embarrassment. Still, many FL professionals hold dear the idea that the classroom locus, the mere physical presence of all participants being in the same time and place, affords students an inherent advantage for language learning (no matter what pedagogy is employed). Beliefs need no proof in order to be widely held and defended; most language professionals continue to be skeptical about the efficacy of students' interacting online precisely for this reason. More to the point would be to recognize that each SLA theory—interactionist and sociocultural—and each instructional format has respective strengths and weaknesses.

In this chapter I have illustrated, especially through an analysis of bimodal chatting, that CMC can play a crucial role in stimulating linguistic interactions in a fashion that produces similar benefits to those generated by face-to-face collaborations. I deliberately present an instructor-learner CMC exchange from the first year to illustrate the feasibility of adding a CMC component and to highlight the instructor's role in this environment. The transcripts reveal that negotiations of meaning are commonplace. Students have ample opportunities to focus their attention on gaps in their interlanguage, direct the flow of their own learning on an equal footing with that of the teacher, and carry out intensive practice of these new structures both in writing and in speech with the real expectation of adding them to their growing L2 grammar. At the intermediate and advanced levels, classroom activities can be complemented by telecollaborations as well.

The benefits of these CMC practices accrue during the early stages of L2 study even with students of low verbal abilities, as Payne and Whitney (2002) have shown in the case of the positive effect that written chat has on the development of oral proficiency (also see Abrams 2003). Bimodal CMC of the sort examined earlier appears to provide another form of glue that helps maintain interest in the subject matter outside of class. These benefits do not automatically or deterministically derive from the tools themselves but rather from how CMC is used in service of promoting meaningful interactions and real intercultural reflections.

Either written and/or voice chat is not without its communicative problems. Breakdowns are frequent, but they also provide golden opportunities for students and teacher alike to focus attention on the emerging L2 system as well as new ways of conceiving of one's bilingual identity. This heightens rather than diminishes the teacher's role in raising awareness and task setting (O'Rourke and Schwienhorst, 2003). Just as the classroom's supposed a priori edge of the here and now can be thoroughly neutralized, or even undermined, by poorly designed activities, successful CMC just doesn't happen because the tool is there—it must be carefully planned. Again, the teacher's initiative is crucial to the success of CMC activities.

Both students and instructors need training in how to profit from bimodal CMC; it is not an activity that comes naturally to most teachers or students. In fact, the bimodal aspects and the persistent problems of time lag can be quite confusing, if not disconcerting, for the first few sessions. The incessant chants of "Can you hear me?" or the frequent written responses of "Are you still there?" clearly attest to some of CMC's inherent difficulties. To say the least, it is not intuitively obvious to even the seasoned language instructor how such a tool must be employed in service of L2 language learning. How technology as a whole can help create a successful learning environment for the distance learning student is the topic of the next chapter.

DISCUSSION QUESTIONS AND ACTIVITIES

1.   What does Kramsch (1993) mean when she says that the goal of L2 students should be to find their own third place?

2.   Describe three situations where asynchronous CMC (e.g., e-mail, e-bulletin boards/forums, blogs, wikis) would be preferred over synchronous CMC.

3.   Go online to the Cultura website (http://web.mit.edu/french/ culturaNEH/), study the materials, and write a two-paragraph summary of the project. Would this framework work for the language you teach? Give reasons why and why not and make specific reference to proficiency levels: first year, second year, third year.

4.   Conduct a survey of your students and colleagues to determine what kinds of CMC tools they use and how frequently. Fill in the chart using the following Likert values:

0 = not at all   3 = several times a week
1 = once a week   4 = relatively frequently during the week
2 = more than once a week   5 = every day

Persons Interviewed	E-mail	e-BB or Forums	Blogs	Wikis	IM or Text Chat	Cell Phone Text Messaging	Chat with Sound
1							
2							
3							
4							

How have these usage patterns changed in the last five years?

5.   Design a jigsaw task for your students to accomplish working in pairs. Each partner should have only part of the knowledge necessary to complete the task to help ensure that the participants work together. Share the task with your colleagues and try it out. What types of FonF or negotiations of meaning do you expect to occur when your students try to accomplish this task?

NOTES

1. For an excellent overview of CMC tools, see Lafford and Lafford (2005).
2. See www.slf.ruhr-uni-bochum.de/index.html.
3. For example, see http://facebook.com.
4. See www.wimba.com.
5. For example, www.blogger.com/start; www.duber.com/oncall/; http://uniblogs .la.psu.edu.
6. See www.skype.com/.
7. See https://skypecasts.skype.com/skypecasts//.html.
8. See www.bjfogg.com/.
9. An additional complication derives from the fact that the personal "*a*" allows for a highly flexible word order, although different pragmatic interpretation can be motivated: "*A mi esposo le gusta la carne*"; "*Le gusta la carne a mi esposo.*"
10. See www.freinet.org.
11. See www.culturacommunity.org/drupal/ or http://web.mit.edu/french/cultura NEH/.

Chapter 5

Distance Learning for Languages

Does It Measure Up?

BACKGROUND

"Do you use technology in your foreign language classroom?" Few language teachers would dare to answer "no" to this leading question for fear of being classified as outdated or out of touch with best practices. Not surprising, most teachers routinely employ web pages to distribute syllabi assignments, cultural materials, webquests, and even lecture notes created in PowerPoint, which can then be automatically converted into web pages. But at the point that the faculty is polled about accepting credit for language courses delivered in a hybrid or entirely distance learning format on an equal footing with classroom instruction, the smiles begin to fade and the positive attitudes toward technology evaporate. Many FL teachers harbor deep-seated doubts as to whether a hybrid course, much less a completely virtual learning experience, could ever provide L2 learners with an accepted way to gain linguistic proficiency, especially when oral language skills are in question. I suspect that many language instructors secretly worry that these new distance learning (DL) classes will displace them or perhaps force them to change their traditional teacher-centered classrooms into educational environments that are more student centered.

Despite these fears, national education trends increasingly include DL classes as a delivery format for all disciplines. Allen and Seaman (2006, 2007) reported that approximately 3.2 million higher-education students, or one in five, were taking at least one course online in fall 2005, which accounted for a 40 percent increase from the previous year; by fall 2006 there were 3.5 million students, or one in six, taking online courses, a 10 percent increase from 2005. They calculate that online learning has a 9.7 percent growth rate versus the 1.5 percent growth experienced in enrollment from the rest of higher education. Most of this expansion occurred in two-year associate institutions, which constitute approximately one-half of all online enrollments, and in the larger, public universities. The principal advantages were access, especially for nontraditional students, and the ability to complete the degree. In terms of quality, the majority of chief academic officers at these institutions felt that the online courses were equivalent or even superior to their face-to-face counterparts. However, faculty acceptance, perceived acceptance in the marketplace, the rigorous demands of independent learning, and the lack of student discipline in the online environment were all cited as important barriers to the implementation of online courses and programs. These online students number overwhelmingly in the undergraduate population and hailed almost exclusively from the larger universities (i.e., fifteen thousand enrollments or more). More than half (51.5%) of the online students are enrolled in two-year associate institutions (6). In terms of quality, 62 percent of the chief academic officers at these large universities felt that the online courses are equivalent or even superior to their face-to-face counterparts. Not surprisingly, faculty acceptance, the demands of learning new teaching methods, and the lack of student discipline in the online learning environment were all cited as the most important barriers to the implementation of online courses and programs.

DL for languages is a complicated subject. On the one hand, there are only a handful of DL language courses being offered for credit in our universities and even fewer evaluation studies available that could be used to establish a strong track record with which to assess their impact and to argue for or against offering students this alternative (Goertler and Winke 2008). On the other hand, no language professional, not even the most technologically enamored instructor or CALL researcher, would dispute the notion that in order to reach advanced proficiency levels (Interagency Language Roundtable Scale [ILR] level 3 or higher), L2 students need to interact face-to-face with native speakers, preferably in a country where the language is spoken. How else could an L2 student develop an appropriate sense of pragmatic and sociolinguistic competence, let alone advance linguistic competence?

Using a student record database maintained by the American Council of Teachers of Russian (ACTR) that spans more than thirty years, Davidson

(2004, 2007) has analyzed the gains in listening, reading, and spoken competency of approximately 3,500 L2 students of Russian who have gone abroad. His results document without any doubt that the gains toward advanced proficiency are due to study abroad—especially when carried out in full-year study programs as opposed to just one semester.[1] Unfortunately, of the 45 percent of entering U.S. freshmen who profess the intent to study abroad, fewer than 3 percent actually undertake it (Davidson 2007). This explains why both administrators and the FL profession obviously need to bring more pressure on the university curriculum to include study abroad as a requirement for graduation.[2]

In this light, perhaps, intercultural CMC projects such as those described in chapter 4 might be used to advantage as a way of whetting beginning-level students' appetite for study abroad by providing direct contact through telecollaboration or text/sound chatting with speakers of the target culture. What role, then, do DL courses have to play in the general FL curriculum? There is probably not a single ideal answer. Critics of learning language at a distance routinely tend to couch the debate in terms of all or nothing—all DL courses versus no DL courses—whereas the real issue is how to obtain the smooth articulation of DL offerings into the overall FL curriculum in ways that accommodate the needs of an institution's learners without compromising quality. In other words, DL language courses should be conceived as part of a diversified path (including study abroad opportunities) that FL departments employ to meet different needs of their students.

A discussion of DL issues could focus on any level, especially when higher levels of literacy come into the picture, but here I examine beginning language instruction via DL to pose the following question: Can a hybrid or a completely virtual format engender linguistic progress comparable to that fostered within a traditional L2 classroom environment that meets five days a week, especially with respect to oral proficiency? This is the heart of the matter for those who doubt the efficacy of the DL learning format. In other words, do DL classes have a role to play in the FL language curriculum, perhaps as one way to begin the journey down the long road to advanced proficiency—a feat, as I discussed in chapter 1, that requires a minimum of 700 to 1,320 hours of instruction? The answer is particularly important in the case of the less commonly taught languages, or LCTLs, where access to beginning instruction is especially limited due to teacher shortages, low enrollments, and the concomitant financial constraints.

Even with respect to a language like Arabic—an LCTL in high demand partly because of the current state of world affairs—the lack of trained classroom teachers puts in jeopardy the chances of meeting national priorities for Arabic language readiness, especially if delivery is limited to the traditional classroom format (Al-Batal 2007). Wiley (2007) has argued for harnessing the power of the diverse language communities or heritage speakers residing in the United States in order to meet the national language priorities in the short run. But in the long run, our educational system also needs to produce more nonheritage Americans who are able to speak Arabic, Farsi, Punjabi, and other LCTLs; in other words, the United States needs to produce more bilinguals from the population of nonheritage learners as well as take advantage of the rich bilingualism that already exists among our increasingly international communities in this country.

The remainder of this chapter will define the different types of DL formats, give a profile of the type of students it attracts, review the existing studies of DL language instruction, and then present a case study of students learning introductory Spanish at a distance through *Spanish without Walls*. This discussion will serve as background for a general discussion of how DL language courses can fit into the FL curriculum and what an instructor needs to know in order to provide a seamless articulation between a department's DL and non-DL courses.

What Is Distance Learning?

The term *distance learning* has been loosely applied to many different types of learning environments including teleconference, hybrid, blended, or virtual (for a recent overview of DL education, see Stickler and Hauck 2006; Goertler and Winke 2008; also see Holmberg, Shelley, and White 2005). Teaching languages through teleconferencing (two-way interactive closed-circuit TV) has the longest track record in the field, although this medium does not relieve either students or instructors of the burden of showing up at some specific time and place (i.e., the campus TV studio or satellite campus studio), not unlike the demands imposed by the classroom. Teleconferencing allows a teacher, usually one of a LCTL, to reach students who might otherwise have no access to instruction. The U.S. Arabic Distance Learning Network based at Montana State University provides an excellent example built on this type of teleconference model and currently serves approximately fifteen small colleges that would not normally have access to Arabic language instruction.[3] For the students this is a felicitous outcome, as their administrators have no immediate plans to add Arabic to the curriculum at these respective institutions.

Without doubt the live TV/video environment is exciting but not without its limitations with respect to issues of interactivity. Laurillard (2002, 103) considers this format to be heavily oriented toward a teacher-driven pedagogy, despite the purely technical capacity for students to participate. Only with great difficulty do students work together using this format in a more autonomous and constructivist manner (Goodfellow et al. 1996). Normally teleconferences are organized around the teacher's delivery of information, much as a lecture with limited group drill activity and interactivity. Nevertheless Fleming, Hiple, and Du (2002, 18–29) describe successful efforts at the University of Hawai'i to incorporate meaningful group and pair activities into their teleconference format.

O'Dowd (2006, 189) separates videoconferencing into three types: teacher to class, student to student, and class to class. All three types of videoconferencing potentially suffer from sound delays, gaps in fluidity in handovers that make the medium critically different from face-to-face interactions, the tendency toward passive viewing, and other logistic problems (O'Dowd 2006, 191–93). Practical difficulties can become formidable obstacles to carrying out successful videoconference projects when implemented among institutions that do not share the same calendar (i.e., semesters vs. quarters) or do not have adequate mechanisms for sharing credit and financial resources.

Ironically, teleconferencing language courses are readily accepted by faculty curricular committees as being equivalent to the classroom experience with little or no justification despite whatever difficulties might exist in duplicating the same learning experience found in communicative language teaching, the gold standard for best practice in the United States (Magnan 2007). This is due, no doubt, to the primacy of the teacher-driven paradigm as the favored mode for FL instructional delivery. In other words, the presence of the teacher via a teleconference video image projected in real time leads the profession to validate the learning experience on a par with what happens in traditional language classrooms. The rest of this chapter concentrates on other types of DL formats that allow for more autonomous learning styles than those afforded by the teleconference format—approaches that could be more aptly described as learning anywhere anytime, a concept that includes asynchronous as well as synchronous online learning.

Hybrid or blended courses combine in-class instruction for part of the week together with independent work the rest of the time that is supported by a combination of dedicated CALL programs, Internet activities, and/or online chatting. Hybrid courses have become popular with administrators and faculty alike because both can identify with the direct control maintained by the instructors, at least during the classroom meetings (usually two or three times a week). Administrators, in particular, recognize the additional financial potential for stretching an institution's expensive human resources (i.e., teaching assistants and lecturers) to the maximum (Scida and Saury 2006). Hybrid courses allow language departments to increase the number of language sections with the same number of instructors without abandoning the face-to-face component that appears to be emblematic as a guarantee of quality (Young 2002). Nevertheless, many hybrid-course teachers tend to view the computer components of this format as only suitable for drill-and-kill, or mechanical grammar practice, so as to free up the classroom meetings for more communicative activities. Scida and Saury (2006, 520) exemplify this attitude concerning the hybrid curriculum: "Our goals for the use of technology were very simple: going back to the 1980s, literature on use of computers in language instruction and other fields have noted the one thing that the computer can do comparable to what a human being can do is *rote exercises or drills* [emphasis added]."

This view of technology, as Scida and Saury clearly state, is tied to a pedagogy spawned in the 1980s, with roots in behaviorism, well before the explosion of Internet use, web pages, and CMC. Hybrid or blended classrooms are not necessarily constrained by this vision of technology, as illustrated by Bañados (2006), whose blended approach to English as an L2 for Chilean students includes (a) dedicated CALL programs, (b) online monitoring, (c) face-to-face EFL teacher-led classes, and (d) conversation classes with native speakers of English both face-to-face and online. In Bañados's (2006, 539) framework both teachers and students are challenged by new roles: teachers are more like guides and collaborators while students must assume a more autonomous participatory status.

With completely virtual language courses, the teachers and students interact exclusively online; there are no face-to-face meetings, which no doubt accounts for some of the negative reactions to DL typically voiced by language faculty, in contrast to the tolerance shown toward the teleconferencing format and the marginal acceptance of hybrid courses. But entirely virtual courses come in all shapes and sizes and encompass different combinations of asynchronous and/or synchronous modes. More often than not, virtual language courses take advantage of the authoring features provided by standardized course management systems (CMS, see chapter 3), such as WebCT, Blackboard, Sakai, or Moodle (Brandl 2005): for instance, archived lessons, web links, multimedia libraries, drop boxes, announcements, internal mail, bulletin boards or discussion forums, wikis, chat tools (synchronous textual exchange and sometimes voice exchanges too), whiteboards, quiz templates, and customized grade books.

Clearly student autonomy constitutes one of the strengths of these different DL formats with the implicit understanding that students are ripe for this challenge. But that is not always the case, as will be discussed in the next section.

Student Demand for DL Classes

Why would anyone want to take a language course that didn't involve five days of class each week? In fact, the DL format is not an appropriate learning environment for everyone; it tends to be self-selecting. A completely virtual course appeals, in particular, to people who work full-time and therefore need special access to instruction, as well as to those who prefer to work independently. The popularity of a hybrid course also responds to these factors but in a somewhat more disjunctive relationship: those who want fewer in-class hours (and some think this means less work too!) or those who like to work independently. Many students belatedly find out that either partial or total DL formats require much more self-motivation and self-discipline than they are willing to give. These factors might explain the usually high dropout rate for the DL learning environment for all disciplines (Carr 2000). Ironically, students with strong motivation to learn LCTLs such as Arabic, Farsi, Filipino, or Punjabi, to name only a few, may find to their dismay that there are no classroom language offerings available locally, making the DL format the only way to get started in these cases. Slowly the FL profession is beginning to respond to this demand for more LCTL instruction.

EVALUATION OF ONLINE LANGUAGE LEARNING

As stated earlier, very little empirical research has yet addressed the overall effectiveness of online language learning or compared the progress of students participating in such courses with that of those enrolled in traditional classes. Likewise, little is known about students' perception of their online learning experience. I have divided the studies that do exist into hybrid courses and entirely distance learning formats, and I also give a brief review of the literature.

Hybrid Courses

To date, most studies of online language learning for beginners have evaluated hybrid courses that combine regular class meetings with computer-mediated instruction. Results indicate that online activities can be substituted for some of the class time normally required in language courses without adversely affecting students' progress. As a whole, they also suggest that students who learn a language online may develop literacy skills that are superior to those of students enrolled in traditional courses (Warschauer 1996).

Two groups of researchers, Adair-Hauck, Willingham-McLain, and Earnest-Youngs (1999) and Green and Earnest-Youngs (2001), compared the achievement test scores of students enrolled in standard elementary French and German classes, respectively, that met four days per week (control group) with the scores of other learners who attended class three days a week and who participated in technologically enhanced learning activities in lieu of a fourth hour of in-class contact (treatment group). Adair-Hauck,

Willingham-McLain, and Earnest-Youngs (1999) found that students participating in the treatment group did as well as those in the control group on tests
of listening, speaking, and cultural knowledge. In addition, these students performed significantly better than the control group on measures of reading and
writing ability. The authors speculate that online students were more motivated to write, but they offer no explanation with respect to the reading results.
In contrast, Green and Earnest-Youngs (2001) found no significant difference
between the scores of the treatment and control groups on the same type of
tests used in the study adapted for the web by Adair-Hauck and colleagues.
Why these two studies report different findings is not immediately clear.

Chenoweth and Murday (2003) examined the outcomes of an elementary
French course, *Elementary French Online*, developed at Carnegie Mellon
University in 2000 and delivered mostly online, along with an hour-long,
face-to-face class meeting once per week as well as weekly twenty-minute individual or small-group meetings with a native speaker tutor. Chenoweth,
Jones, and Tucker (2006) provide an update on the project that includes a
Spanish counterpart, *Spanish Online Learning*, to the French hybrid course.
The progress of French and Spanish L2 students in the online group was
compared to that of others who attended a traditional class four hours per
week on tests of oral production, listening comprehension, reading comprehension, grammar knowledge, and written production. The results showed
that the scores for the treatment and control groups were not significantly
different for oral production and only slightly different for the writing samples, with essays by students in the online group being judged superior to
those of the control group on a variety of measures including grammatical
accuracy and syntactic complexity (Chenoweth, Jones, and Tucker 2006,
158–59). All students were weakest in the use of transitions and general essay
organization. Likewise, other measures for listening comprehension, grammar knowledge, and reading comprehension registered minimal statistical
differences. The first study also found that the online students spent approximately one hour per week less studying than did those in the traditional
class, suggesting that the online course was more efficient because students
achieved results similar to those attained by learners in the conventional class
with less time expenditure. But the second study that included the Spanish
course showed that students spent an equal amount of time regardless of
learning format (e.g., 8.5 hours per week).

Nieves (1996) reported on the performance of students enrolled in *Éxito* (Federal Language Training Laboratory, 1990), an introductory Spanish course in a format very similar to that of the online French program in the study by Chenoweth and Murday (2003). The *Éxito* program was the basis for a survival Spanish course developed for government employees. It was originally a ten-day course with each day devoted to learning to survive in Spanish with regard to some aspect of daily life such as ordering meals, getting driving directions, and so on. Nieves expanded it into a semester-long course in which students worked with the materials primarily on their own and attended a one-hour face-to-face class meeting per week. Besides the video newscast, the other multimedia components were audiocassettes and graphics. There were no web-based activities, as the study was done in 1994 when the web was not yet widely employed in language teaching. Nieves used her own set of outcome listening measures to show that students who participated in the multimedia-based course outperformed those enrolled in traditional courses on measures of aural and oral communication skills but scored slightly lower on a test of writing ability.

Finally, another group of researchers (Scida and Saury 2006; Epps 2004; Walczynski 2002; Echávez-Solano 2003) followed the progress of students using *Mallard*, a drill/quiz exercise and tracking program designed and supported by the University of Illinois (Champaign-Urbana). In general, these four studies show no significant differences among the experimental (*Mallard*) group and the control group, with Scida and Saury's (2006) study registering slightly higher final grades for the group using *Mallard*. These researchers attributed much of the student success with the Mallard program to students' ability to continue working on the exercises until reaching 100 percent accuracy. In essence, the availability of the tutorial CALL program allowed students to dedicate more time to making more automatic their control of the basic language structures.

To summarize, the studies described earlier provide limited evidence that the hybrid online format can contribute to FL learning but that a great deal depends on the learning environment, pedagogical materials, and tasks. Because some of these studies combine online instruction with face-to-face class meetings, it is difficult to generalize their results to language courses conducted entirely online. Specifically, it should be noted, however, that while the regular small-group meetings with instructors in the online French course studied by Chenoweth and Murday (2003) or in the *Éxito* program benefited the students, they complicate the interpretation of outcome data because such opportunities for intimate interaction with fluent speakers of the target language are rarely available in any introductory language class, either conventional or online.

Courses Taught Entirely Online

Thus far, only three studies (Cahill and Catanzaro 1997; Soo and Ngeow 1998; Blake and Delforge 2005) have evaluated language courses taught entirely online using empirical data. In both cases online learners were found to outperform students in conventional courses on the grammar output measures.

Cahill and Catanzaro (1997) reported on an introductory online Spanish class that might be considered somewhat low-tech, as it did not have a multimedia component. The *Dos Mundos* textbook (Terrell et al. 2002) along with the accompanying audiocassettes and lab manual were used as the core course materials. Online activities included synchronous chat sessions, open-ended web assignments, practice tests, and a substantial number of pen-pal writing assignments. Responses to two essay questions were used to compare the progress of students participating in the experimental group to that of students enrolled in conventional Spanish classes. Based on ratings of global quality and percentage error scores, the writing samples of students in the online course were judged to be significantly better than those in the traditional classes. Although not discussed by the authors, it seems clear that more writing was demanded of the online students, thereby making it hard to ascertain whether this effect was due solely to the online teaching format.

Soo and Ngeow (1998) compared the performance of 77 students enrolled in conventional English classes with 111 students who studied English exclusively through a multimedia CALL program. A comparison of pre- and posttest TOEFL scores showed that students in the online group not only made significantly greater improvement than those in conventional classes but also did it in a shorter period of time, as the experimental course was five weeks shorter due to technical difficulties.

As is the case for the hybrid courses reviewed earlier, the results from these two studies suggest that online language learning can be effective, at least as a means of improving writing, reading, and listening comprehension abilities. But these studies did not explain why the online environment produced these results, and more research is needed to substantiate these initial observations. Cahill and Catanzaro's (1997) results must be viewed with caution, as it could easily be argued that the reason distance students wrote better final essays was simply a function of the large amount of writing practice.

Blake and Delforge (2005) have provided additional data for Spanish learners based on discrete grammar exams. Their results show that DL students often perform significantly better than their classroom counterparts, but many research difficulties mitigate the strength of these and other findings. As is the case with much research in the second SLA field, more data points for DL learners would make findings like Blake and Delforge's more reassuring (Thompson and Hiple 2005). Unfortunately, DL students are particularly recalcitrant when it comes to responding to requests for cooperation outside the boundaries of class assignments. After all, with virtual students, there is no physical presence in the first place; these students are too busy working or doing other things. Classroom researchers tend to have more luck getting in situ students to cooperate, perhaps because they are a captured audience.

Finally, the burden of isolating the experimental treatment so as to focus on the medium alone (DL vs. classroom instruction), to the exclusion of all other factors, remains a daunting, if not insurmountable, challenge. Much of the research done in comparing student outcomes between traditional classroom delivery and the DL environment in all disciplines has given rise to no significant differences (Russell 2001). Again, one of the difficulties in this line of research is isolating the format variable from all of the other factors that contribute to L2 learning outcomes—for example, learner characteristics, instructional method, and media attributes. One might even say that this type of research, medium comparison studies, is inherently flawed as it is not grounded in examining the premises and/or predictions of any particular theory of learning (Pedersen 1987; Horn 1992; Burston 2006). After all, students learning a second language in whatever format have to do a great deal of language practice, which tends to level the performance outcomes for everyone. Nevertheless, both administrators and the profession at large continue to demand these types of comparative studies because of their fundamental distrust of technologically assisted formats.

Students' Perceptions of the Online Learning Experience

A handful of studies have asked students to describe and rate the quality of their experience in online language classes (Adair-Hauck, Willingham-McLain, and Earnest-Youngs, 1999; Chenoweth and Murday, 2003; Green and Earnest-Youngs, 2001).

Adair-Hauck, Willingham-McLain, and Earnest-Youngs (1999) used a self-report questionnaire to compare the attitudes and opinions of students in their hybrid French course with those of students taking a conventional class. They found that a higher percentage of students in the hybrid class reported meeting their personal language-learning goals over the course of the semester than did those in the traditional class. A number of students in the technology-enhanced class also indicated that the flexibility of the multimedia materials contributed to their progress in the class, noting the advantage of being able to spend more time on activities they found particularly difficult; in short, there was more student-centered learning. This is not to say that student-driven materials cannot be incorporated into the regular classroom but rather that students often perceive that the classroom is teacher driven as opposed to the student-driven nature of the online format.

Responses to a self-report questionnaire administered to online and offline students by Green and Earnest-Youngs (2001) and the results of course evaluations collected by Chenoweth and Murday (2003) shed a less positive light on the online language learning experience. Students in the hybrid and conventional courses studied by Green and Earnest-Youngs (2001) reported equal levels of satisfaction with the progress they had achieved. However, students who completed web-based activities in place of a fourth hour of class time found some web pages too difficult and some of the activities not sufficiently well organized. The mostly online French course evaluated by Chenoweth and Murday (2003) received a lower overall rating on student evaluations than did a conventional class taken by learners in the control group. The authors note that the low course ratings may be due to factors other than its technological component, because students' complaints dealt with organization and grading.

Murray (1999) also reported on students' assessment of their experiences learning language with CALL materials. He interviewed Canadian university students who used an interactive videodisc program to study

French for one semester and obtained responses that were very similar to those found by Adair-Hauck, Willingham-McLain, and Earnest-Youngs (1999). For example, students in Murray's study commented that they liked the ability to work at their own pace and focus their efforts on activities that were particularly difficult for them, indicating once again the benefit of student-directed learning. In addition, a number of students stated that they found that working independently with the videodisc materials caused them less anxiety than participating in a conventional language class.

Notwithstanding the limited amount of research available at this time, students' reactions to the experience of learning language online seem to be mostly positive. Students appreciate the flexibility afforded by CALL materials and their potential for self-directed learning. Murray's (1999) results also indicate that working with CALL may make language learning less stressful for some students.

The FL profession, however, is now more concerned with oral proficiency than with discrete grammar tests or even attitudes, undoubtedly as a result of the dominant role accorded to the American Council on the Teaching of Foreign Languages (ACTFL) Oral Proficiency Interviews (OPI), the primary means for assessment at present, although it is not without its critics (Kramsch 1986), who fault this evaluation procedure for its limited conception of what knowing another language and culture is suppose to mean. The following case study is an attempt to add more empirical data concerning the development of oral proficiency among the language DL population.

ORAL PROFICIENCY AND E-LEARNING: THE CASE OF SPANISH WITHOUT WALLS

Both hybrid and DL formats understandably raise concerns as to whether these learning environments can provide adequate practice in speaking.[4] In response to this worry, I present a detailed account of oral assessment that was carried out with students enrolled in traditional, hybrid, and DL first-year Spanish courses. The assessment instrument consisted of an automated phone test, the Versant for Spanish test developed by Harcourt Assessment.[5] The Versant test is based on Levelt's (1989) construct of oral proficiency that requires students to listen, repeat, and/or respond. The scoring is done without human intervention using automatic voice-recognition software and a Spanish parser (Bernstein et al. 2004). The findings, reported in more detail later, support the notion that hybrid and DL instruction allow students to develop comparable levels of oral proficiency during the first year of study. The results also suggest that the currently available proficiency testing measures—such as ACTFL's OPI, the Interagency Linguistic Roundtable Oral Proficiency Interview (ILR/OPI), the Common European Framework exam (CEF), and even Versant's Spanish Spoken Test—are less successful at teasing out different proficiency levels among first-year students with fewer than two hundred hours of instruction (i.e., the first four quarters of university L2 instruction) but more successful at broadly differentiating between first-year oral performance and that of the intermediate level. In other words, present testing instruments register a demonstrable jump in abilities at the intermediate level (ILR level 1 or CEF level B) for all students—traditional, hybrid, and DL.

Curricular Content for Spanish without Walls

The *Spanish without Walls* (SWW) courses (Van de Pol 2001) provide a first-year Spanish curriculum in both a hybrid format with three hours' face-to-face instruction two days per week in addition to six hours of study via technology, and a completely virtual format where instructors and students never meet in person. The first-year course, whether in the hybrid or DL format, combines multimedia language materials from three sources:

- *Tesoros*, a five-disk tutorial CD-ROM detective story (Blake, Blasco, and Hernández 2001)
- Content-based web readings and Flash activities
- A collaborative CMC tool running on the Flash communications server that allows for both asynchronous and synchronous textual written communication in addition to half-duplex (i.e., walkie-talkie) sound exchange

The five CD-ROMs served as the course textbook.[6] The remaining online materials were packaged into a Moodle course management system designed to teach first-year Spanish grammar and vocabulary, provide exercises, conduct testing, present authentic Spanish-language multimedia materials, and enable oral communication with teachers and peers.

Students alternated between use of the CD-ROMs and the SWW website to cover the scope and sequence of a normal university Spanish language course. This is a clear blending of the use of computer as tool (CMC) and computer as tutor (CD-ROM) that Hubbard and Siskin (2004) have suggested as an ideal way of implementing CALL (see chapter 3). Students were held accountable for the *Tesoros* CD-ROM material by means of online exams that covered the vocabulary, story line, and grammar presented therein. Students were also required to chat live with their instructor in groups of no more than three at least once a week for one hour and several more times with their assigned partners, as time and schedules permitted, in order to complete the collaborative content-based tasks. For example, one student would research the capital cities of four Latin American countries, while his or her partner would investigate the same type of information for four other countries. During the chat the students would share their results with each other and then summarize the findings in either a joint or individual composition.

The hybrid courses (SPA 2V and 3V) are the equivalent of the last two-thirds of an introductory college-level Spanish course delivered in a hybrid course format. The curriculum is derived from *Spanish without Walls*; students meet with their instructor for three hours, two days a week, and then perform web activities and CMC synchronous dialogues using Macromedia's Breeze (which provides text chat, VoIP, and whiteboard/character-by-character text exchange). The course materials and exercises focus on developing the same array of skills promoted in the classroom courses, Spanish 2 and Spanish 3, and provide students with exposure to a variety of Spanish accents from Spain and Latin America and extensive reading knowledge of authentic texts, guided writing practice, the second part of first-year grammar and vocabulary sequence, and cultural awareness of the Spanish-speaking world.

Measuring Proficiency: Versant for Spanish Test

In Levelt's (1989) model, both speaking and listening activate similar processing modules, although only one mode, speaking, specifically involves articulation. But in all other terms of processing, Levelt contends that speaking and listening activate identical mechanisms. Accordingly, the Versant Spanish phone test asks participants to read aloud, listen and repeat, say the opposite, answer short questions, build sentences from jumbled-up word combinations, answer open questions, and retell stories. The responses from test takers for all but the last two categories are scored automatically by means of a speech recognition and parser program informed by data from a large corpus of native speakers ($n=435$) from a variety of Spanish-speaking countries as well as L2 learners of Spanish ($n=579$; Bernstein et al. 2004). The Versant algorithm divides the linguistic data into separate values for vocabulary, sentence mastery, pronunciation, and fluency and then combines these values in order to come up with an overall score on a scale from 20 to 80.

Most important, the results from the Versant test demonstrate a close correlation with the human-scored OPI, the ILR/OPI, and the CEF exams ($r=0.86$, $r=0.90$, and $r=0.92$, respectively;[7] see Bernstein et al. 2004, 4). This means that the twenty-minute phone sample provides sufficient data with which the algorithm can identify the oral proficiency of the speaker, for all intents and purposes, as well as human judges are able to do so using the protocols developed by the ACTFL, ILR, and CEF.

For doing assessment research with DL students, who are hard to track down in the first place, the Versant test is particularly advantageous because the participants can take it anywhere in the world, at a time of their own choosing, by calling a toll-free number. The fact that the Versant exam takes approximately twenty minutes to complete further heightens its attractiveness as a research instrument in the DL context.

Student Population

During 2005–6, the Versant instrument was administered to 233 University of California traditional classroom students from the eight levels of the lower division curriculum.[8] This population consisted of the first seven quarters of Spanish language instruction along with one class of heritage speakers enrolled in a special lower-division language series designed for native speakers. Heritage learners (HL) constitute an extremely heteroge-

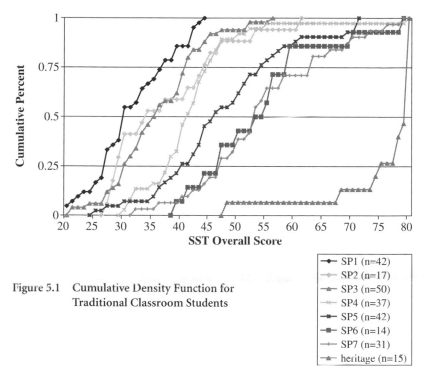

Figure 5.1   Cumulative Density Function for
Traditional Classroom Students

some HL students have distinct oral advantages over non-HL students, they also tend to lack competence with academic Spanish or the more formal registers (see Blake and Zyzik 2003). There really is no such thing as one HL linguistic profile but a continuum of heritage learners with varying linguistic strengths. Nevertheless I predicted that the HL students would strongly outperform the non-HL students on the Versant measure, an expectation that was confirmed by the results (see figure 5.1).

With this robust baseline for the traditional classroom students serving as a norm, I compared these classroom Versant test scores against those of the additional sixty-five hybrid and twenty-one DL learners to categorize them as ahead, behind, or equal to the traditional classroom trends—much as a placement test does. In this fashion I developed a range of scores that demonstrate the relative efficacy of the DL format without minimizing the problems of individual differences that plague most SLA studies (Skehan 1989).

Results and Discussion

Figure 5.1 displays the Versant test scores by level for the traditional classroom learners as a function of their respective cumulative densities: In other words, each Versant test value is matched to the proportional number of students from that group who have reached that score or below. Accordingly, a graph of cumulative densities reveals group trends while at the same time accurately portrays individual differences. In any given group or class, some students will score very high and some very low on the Versant exam. What is important to know is how many of the students score very high or very low and at what point their scores group together (i.e., their cumulative densities). A class with a low percentage of students scoring 35 or below on the Versant exam signals a group not as advanced as a class with a large percentage of students scoring 35 or below. (Note that the percentage is the most important element in a cumulative density graph, not the total number of students above and below a score of 35, which will vary.) In this fashion, the cumulative density graph captures group trends without erasing the range of individual differences, which are to be expected when dealing with data in SLA research.

Given the range of language proficiency among these eight levels, one would expect to see the Versant values varying according to the amount of completed quarters of language study, which is what the results in figure 5.1 confirm. Students with one to four quarters of Spanish study cluster together (with the fourth quarter representing a transitional phase to more advanced capabilities), in contrast to other students with five to seven quarters of study, who also appear to form a separate group. The heritage students belong in a group by themselves due to their very advanced test scores. This visual impression was statistically confirmed by means of a Tukey Honestly Significant Difference (HSD) test, the standard statistical measure to apply when no a priori hypotheses exist with respect to group differences (see appendix for more complete statistical treatment).

The range of scores, after norming the data by eliminating the 10th and 90th percentiles, can be summarized as follows:

COURSE NUMBER	VERSANT SCORE
Courses 1, 2, and 3	25–40
Course 4	31–49
Courses 5, 6, and 7	37–68

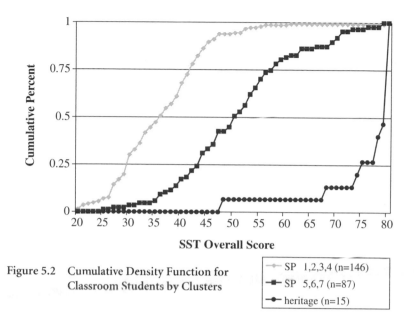

Figure 5.2   Cumulative Density Function for Classroom Students by Clusters

SP 1,2,3,4 (n=146)
SP 5,6,7 (n=87)
heritage (n=15)

These facts are visually captured in figure 5.2, where the cumulative density functions have been plotted after pooling the data into these three distinct groups in order to highlight the differences in oral proficiency that occurs after the fourth quarter of language study. In terms of oral proficiency, the heritage students, not unexpectedly, outperformed all of the nonheritage groups.

Figure 5.3 plots the cumulative density function for all learners (total $n = 334$): classroom ($n = 233$), hybrid ($n = 65$), and virtual ($n = 21$). In figure 5.3 notice that the DL students clearly follow the trends set by the first-year+ group of classroom learners. The hybrid learners are performing only slightly less well at the higher end than the first-year+ group, but remember that the traditional group includes students from the fourth quarter too, which should logically give them an added edge. The totally DL students performed slightly better than the classroom students from the first-year+ group, although the individual t tests (see appendix) revealed no significant differences between either the hybrid or completely DL learners and their respective classroom counterparts (i.e., the first-quarter DL students

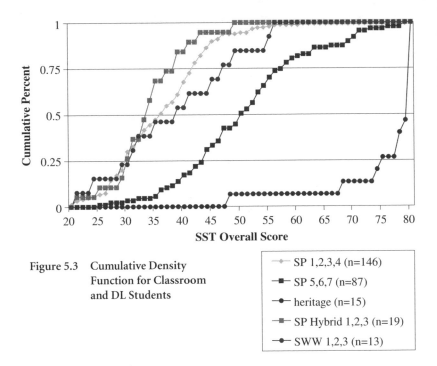

Figure 5.3   Cumulative Density
Function for Classroom
and DL Students

SP 1,2,3,4 (n=146)	
SP 5,6,7 (n=87)	
heritage (n=15)	
SP Hybrid 1,2,3 (n=19)	
SWW 1,2,3 (n=13)	

compared to classroom first-quarter students, and the second-quarter DL students compared to classroom second-quarter students, etc.).

The number of distance learners ($n=21$) who took the Versant exam is, again, limited because there is no way to follow up with students who have never attended a class session in person. This obvious shortcoming, however, is somewhat mitigated by the strength of the baseline results: The large baseline corpus establishes a placement norm against which each individual hybrid or DL student's score can be compared and then located in a curricular space. Viewed from this relative perspective, both types of e-learning formats have allowed students to develop levels of oral proficiency that are commensurate with the expectations for the in-class traditional learners. In other words, the online and hybrid formats also permit students to develop speaking skills that are in line with the expected norms for the first year.

Pinpointing which specific factors are responsible for putting the virtual students on an equal footing with their classroom counterparts is not an easy task. In the first place, the DL students in the SWW course are older, more mature, and more self-motivated than their younger classroom counterparts—virtual courses tend to self-select, as I have already discussed. These L2 learners are, undoubtedly, more efficient, autonomous, and responsible as they pay in advance for the DL course and they cannot afford to waste either their money or time. Those potential DL learners who do not possess these qualities tend to drop out at the beginning. One might expect that hybrid students would follow suit, but many students have enrolled in the hybrid course expressly to take advantage of the reduced class time; in other words, some are actively avoiding work. For their part, the traditional classroom students often project a self-satisfied attitude based merely on their showing up for class five days a week. It comes as no surprise that some classroom learners make little additional efforts outside of class to study the L2.

No doubt the required synchronous chat sessions in the two DL formats, which tend to provide students with even more individual attention from the instructor than is humanly possible in a fifty-minute class with twenty-five to thirty students, directly contributed to their relatively comparable performances on the Versant measure. The profession is just beginning to study how to most effectively utilize these CMC tools (see chapter 4) within the context of either a DL or a traditional language course.

The results from this case study have further implications that the FL profession needs to take stock of. Classroom students for the first year+ (less than two hundred hours of instruction) do not seem to make that much noticeable progress with respect to oral proficiency despite the current emphasis on oral proficiency and with the OPI as the main tool for assessment. In part, this appears to be due to the plateau-like L2 development pattern that has emerged as well from the SWW study and its findings. The *ILR rating scale* acknowledges implicitly this first-year plateau or, at least, takes it into account by classifying those students with fewer than two hundred hours of instruction as "zero" or "zero-plus" speakers. But what does "zero-plus" mean, if the speaker is still a "zero"? This zero label sticks with the L2 examinee for most of those first two hundred hours, right up to the fourth quarter of college instruction, which understandably led ACTFL to propose a new set of user-friendly rubrics such as "novice low," "novice mid," "novice high." The CEF refers to levels A, B, and C. Being a novice or an A-1 definitely sounds better than being a zero, but the development pattern remains essentially the same. These labels capture the same insight gained in the SWW case study where students appear to make progress very slowly until they reach the two-hundred-hour threshold level, whether graded by human interviewers or by an automated exam such as Versant. The first two hundred hours truly belong to that zone referred to as interlanguage. Obviously, beginning students are making significant progress along the way, but it's difficult to calibrate with the existing assessment tools. Distinguishing small degrees of change in oral proficiency among L2 students with fewer than two hundred hours remains a clear challenge for the assessment field in the future.

No one would be as foolish as to suggest that DL e-learning alone could therefore be used exclusively in place of face-to-face contact to reach advanced proficiency (i.e., 3+ on the ILR scale). Rather this case suggests that the DL format should be considered as one legitimate learning avenue among many others, including study abroad, within the context of diversified FL instructional program.

IMPLEMENTING LANGUAGE INSTRUCTION AT A DISTANCE: LESSONS LEARNED

The *Spanish without Walls* experience and the reports from other online efforts documented by the Sloan Consortium (Moore 2004) suggest the following guidelines to offering online language instruction:[9]

- Orient students on how to learn online and help them adjust to their new role as more self-directed and independent learners.
- Write clear learning objectives at both the macro (i.e., syllabus) and micro (i.e., day-by-day) levels of curricular planning.
- Ensure that the quality of the online course is comparable to that of traditional classroom materials.
- Provide ready help in both technical and content issues and respond within twenty-four hours (or sooner, if possible).

- Minimize technical difficulties for obtaining the necessary plug-ins and software.
- Feature interaction—with instructors, classmates, and the interface—at all possible moments.
- Include student feedback in shaping the instructional goals for specific activities (see Laurillard's *conversational framework* as discussed in chapter 6).
- Recycle instruction, materials, topics, concepts, and practice through the course.
- Allow students to practice before oral exams to ensure positive outcomes.
- Demonstrate to students in palpable ways the progress being made throughout the course.

Remember that with completely virtual courses there is no *there* there: Students are not physically present at any time. Even teleconferencing offers a live image of students, which is reassuring in human terms. As a consequence of this, online learning must compensate with increased opportunities for interactions using the CMC tools discussed in chapter 4. The interface design should also give the sense of interactivity whenever possible (see Reeves and Nass 1996; and Fogg 2003).

DL LANGUAGE LEARNING: NOW AND FOR THE FUTURE

The FL profession should not lose sight of the fact that attaining advanced proficiency (ILR level 3) is a most arduous task that requires five or more years of college instruction and critically depends on the nature of the language involved. Languages such as Arabic, Korean, Japanese, and Chinese that have been classified as group IV languages in terms of their learning difficulties (McGinnis 1994) require more hours of instruction than do the Romance languages to reach the same proficiency level, especially given the complexities of their respective writing systems. Yet advanced proficiency is precisely where the nation should want to go, especially in this post–September 11 era, given the urgent need to develop a national language capacity in some of the more strategic LCTLs (Blake and Kramsch 2007).[10] In order to get there, no method of language instruction should be privileged or discarded, although a well-articulated and prolonged study-abroad component along the way might well be a hard-and-fast requirement, as Davidson's (2004, 2007) research has shown.

The current interest in the DL formats, then, must be situated within this context: (a) L2 students need access, (b) students need to work at it for a long time, and (c) students need to study abroad. A DL course is only one piece in this equation but an important avenue to afford students access to introductory instruction of LCTLs when local classroom options are lacking. The increasing number of DL studies should—including the case study of *Spanish without Walls* described earlier—offer the FL profession the comforting knowledge that adding a DL component as a curricular option is a responsible and reasonable format of language instruction, with similar benefits of oral proficiency as those produced in traditional classrooms.

In the case of *Spanish without Walls*, those wedded to in-person OPI exams will no doubt quibble with Versant's construct of oral proficiency while others will note that not enough DL students have been tested to provide conclusive proof. Conclusive proof in the social sciences, including linguistics, is a very elusive goal. The present findings should, at the bare minimum, pique the interest of even the most cynical language professions. Certainly, students will continue to self-select for the type of language instruction they prefer whenever possible. Having options should never be considered a disadvantage to the long-term process of language learning.

The profession should concern itself with providing legitimate options and increasing all avenues of access to language instruction, especially where LCTL instruction is concerned. The DL format can respond effectively to the challenges of best practices in language delivery (Keeton 2004, 86–87): namely, the need to tailor the curriculum to individual student readiness and potential, to make learning goals and paths clear, to link inquiries to genuine problems to enhance motivation, and to provide prompt constructive feedback.

The SWW project in both hybrid and DL formats represents a successful experiment in providing options for Spanish, an overenrolled language spoken widely in U.S. communities (Wiley 2007). The ten campuses that comprise the University of California system are presently engaged in other projects for providing DL language instruction in Arabic from the Berkeley campus and in Punjabi from the Santa Barbara campus.[11] Both projects have received funding from the Department of Education (the Fund for the Improvement of Postsecondary Education [FIPSE] and International Research and Studies [IRS] programs, respectively). Unlike Spanish, both Arabic and Punjabi represent LCTLs, or underenrolled languages, with formidable writing problems: Arabic because of the four ways of writing each letter (initial, medial, final, and in isolation), in addition to the right to left processing and linking requirements; and Punjabi due to the dual scripts, Gurmukhi (Sanskrit based) and Shahmukhi (Persian/Arabic based). Using software and programming that respect the Unicode conventions has simplified most of the potential problems for conducting a DL course in languages like these.

The real challenge, however, lies in implementing DL language instruction within a sound pedagogical framework, a truly conversational framework, as Laurillard (2002, 23) has named it, that seeks "to persuade students to change the way they experience the world through an understanding of the insights of others," blending experiential and formal knowledge. This formidable task is academic in nature and most properly should reside under the purview of those in the FL profession. I have endeavored throughout this book to argue that while technology requires knowledge of new tools (which are constantly changing; see myth 3, *Today's technology is all I need to know*), it is the language instructors, not the technology, that stand in the way of adopting new paradigms and pedagogies. The FL teachers themselves, not the medium, will ultimately determine whether e-learning will make a positive contribution to the L2 student's long march to advanced proficiency. Whether in the context of the classroom or distance learning, each teacher has to learn to give sway to teacher centeredness in favor of a more student-centered and student-autonomous paradigm.

In the process of making the change to this new learning paradigm, both teachers and students must learn to cultivate what Selber (2004) has called a rhetorical computer literacy. This new rhetoric must proceed from what has been the FL profession's solid base: the communicative language teaching, but more in the sense that Hymes (1974) originally meant it—a socially constructed notion that changes the student into a bilingual and bicultural individual as defined uniquely by the individual's own context and experiences (Magnan 2007). This is what Kramsch (1993, 236) means when she refers to students' constantly needing to resituate themselves and their cultural identity in a third place, somewhere between two monolingual idealizations, one defined by the students' mother tongue and the other by the problematic concept of the native speaker. What that new pedagogy consists of and how to get there with the assistance of technology is the topic of the final chapter.

DISCUSSION QUESTIONS AND ACTIVITIES

1.   Discuss whether you would accept credit from another institution that taught your particular language in an online format and explain why.

2.   Make a list of the requirements needed to succeed in a DL course from both the student's and the instructor's point of view.

3.   Imagine that you are teaching a language class online to first-year students. Assume that these students are computer savvy (which is, of course, a big assumption). Design a step-by-step lesson plan for teaching them the present tense with a certain verb using an array of technological tools such as web pages, CALL exercises (e.g., Hot Potatoes), blogs, wikis, and synchronous chat with voice. Would your lesson plan proceed from one tool to the next? In a linear fashion? What tasks would you have the students carry out by themselves? With each other? With you? How could any of these lesson plans be useful for the classroom setting?

4.   Imagine that you are teaching a second-year language class in the classroom. You have students who took the first-year course online and others who were in a classroom. List the strengths and weaknesses that each of these types of students would have. What adjustments would you have to make in order to mesh these two populations together smoothly?

5.   Evaluate how crucial the use of chat with voice is to the success of an online course.

6.   Defend or refute the following statement: "Distance learning language classes are appropriate for all language students."

NOTES

1. For earlier work on this topic, also see Brecht, Davidson, and Ginsberg (1995).
2. See Lincoln Commission Report at www.nafsa.org/public_policy.sec/public _policy_document/study_abroad_1/lincoln_commission_report.
3. See www.arabicstudies.edu/index.shtm.
4. The *Spanish without Walls* project was funded by a three-year FIPSE grant, P116B000315, and produced by co-PIs Robert Blake (University of California, Davis) and María Victoria González Pagani (University of California, Santa Cruz). For a brief description of the project, see http://ittimes.ucdavis.edu/mar2001/blake.html.
5. See http://harcourtassessment.com/haiweb/Cultures/en-US/Harcourt/Community/PostSecondary/Products/Versant/VersantHome.htm.
6. *Tesoros* is now available both as a DVD and as an online course from Boecillo Editora Multimedia; see www.tesoros.es.
7. When the correlation coefficient *r* approaches 1.0, there exists a strong correlation between Versant's results and those of the various oral proficiency tests. Conversely, when *r* approaches 0.0, few or only weak correlations exist. Accordingly, the *r* value indicates a very strong correlation between Versant's results and that of the other human-graded exams.
8. I wish to acknowledge the invaluable help of Cristina Pardo Ballester and María Cetto in the data collection phase of the project.
9. See www.sloan-c.org/effective/.
10. For instance, examine the description of the National Flagship Language Initiative program (www.thelanguageflagship.org) and the National Language Conference (2004; www.nlconference.org) where the need for more national linguistic capacity is laid out in clear strategic terms.
11. See http://uccllt.ucdavis.edu; http://169.237.245.74/aww/info.html; and http://uccllt.ucdavis.edu/distancelearning.cfm. Other teleconference efforts are well underway in Danish, Swedish, and Filipino. See UCLA's World Language Center at www.international.ucla.edu/languages/.

Chapter 6

Putting It All Together

COMMON THREADS

With the publication of *Brave New Schools*, Cummins and Sayers (1995) challenged the language-teaching profession to radically rethink, if not transform, the FL curriculum using global learning networks along the lines of Freinet's (1994) classic dialogic approach. Throughout this book on technology and language teaching, I have either explicitly or implicitly been advocating these and similar steps, albeit from a slightly less sweeping framework, by stressing certain pedagogical threads that should guide the integration of technology into the FL curriculum:

- Multiple technological entry points (web pages and exercises, CALL applications, CD-ROMs/DVDs, CMC, hybrid courses, DL courses)
- Emphasis on how new technologies are used in support of a given theory of SLA, not on what specific tool is being used
- Student-centered classrooms
- Interactivity, agency, and students as (co-)producers of technologically enhanced materials
- Pursuit of a third place in the quest for bilingualism and the development of intercultural communicative competence

In the following sections I review each of these themes separately.

Multiple Technological Entry Points

In chapter 1 (see myth 1) I stress that the term *technology* must be seen as an overarching concept that refers to an array of electronic tools that can be harnessed to assist humans in carrying out certain activities without implying

130

any particular hierarchical ranking. That means that there exists no single best technological tool, just as there is no single pedagogical approach that everyone should follow. Consequently it should not be said that teachers who employ chat programs—for example, either with their students or with students from the target countries—are inherently superior to those CALL practitioners who only use web pages or those who use e-mail only among members of their own classes. Each technique has its own appropriate time and place. Some teachers may feel comfortable using a relatively simple set of technological tools while others will plunge headfirst into using all possibilities, with or without any sense of what they are doing; personalities and teaching styles will differ widely. Nevertheless a successful deployment of technology in service of the FL curriculum will also involve thinking through the entire process and planning carefully.

It is worth reminding ourselves that today's FL curriculum encompasses not only the time spent in class (ten hours at the very most and, more likely, five or less per week) but also the effort spent outside the classroom working in groups (with or without contact with the target speech community at large), as well as all those moments of the night and day spent alone, quietly studying the target language. Again, one tool does not fit all times and places; rather all available tools—web pages, CALL applications, CD ROMs/DVDs, LMS/CMS, synchronous or asynchronous CMC, and whatever new technologies are soon to appear—have a proper place given a felicitous set of learning conditions created by the teacher, supported by the learning environment, and accepted by the learners.

Although I have mostly argued here (see chapter 3) for using a type of CALL that goes beyond the drill-and-kill model, the time alone spent studying a language through drills might be well motivated with an appropriately designed CALL application, as Hubbard and Bradin Siskin (2004) have argued. Steady improvements in feedback routines afforded by advances in iCALL (see chapter 3) will surely continue to heighten a new sense of worth for tutorial CALL.

From another viewpoint, no one should think that the mere use of technology by itself would create educational change in the FL classroom and improve the curriculum (see chapter 1, myth 2). In other words, technology is not a self-determining agent (Selber 2004, 8); only social forces (i.e., teachers and students working together) can create curriculum change and innovation. Nevertheless, tools of all kinds facilitate and encourage the performance of particular activities over others (i.e., *affordances*), and technology can rarely be said to be entirely free of ideological content or to be completely transparent, as computer engineers are prone to describe highly effective computer tools and interfaces. Sociocultural researchers, quite rightly, reject altogether the notion that tools are transparent; they focus on the social structures and the cultures of use/practice that technological tools help reinforce (Thorne 2003; van Dijk 2005).

Ironically, computer engineers can only discover which tools are transparent by letting users *use* them and then observing the results. Consequently, both positions—technology conceived of only as a tool versus technology as a cultural artifact that reflects the discursive, cultural, economic, and geographical systems of power—share the basic notion that one cannot separate the tool from how it's used or embedded in social interactions and institutions. How technology is used should always be the focus and the testing ground for the brave new digital classroom.

Not *What* Technology but *How* It Is Used

The consequences of realizing that tools are not self-determining agents means that *how* any given technological tool is used far outweighs the importance of which tool is selected to carry out a particular activity. Following Chapelle's (2001) earlier example, I have stressed the use of technology in service of a vision of SLA tied to negotiations of meaning, according to the *interactionist hypothesis* (Long and Robinson 1998). Although the interactionist hypothesis may not be the definitive word concerning SLA theoretical discussions, it surely represents one of the most cogent frameworks for research and praxis that the field enjoys at present (Doughty and Long 2003b).

Adopting this general framework is not to suggest that tutorial CALL has no place in the FL curriculum or that it cannot strive to make its exercises as meaningful as possible, a worthy goal even if the format does not immediately lend itself to practice that stimulates negotiations of meaning. Nor should the negotiation-of-meaning approach lead us to a reductionistic classroom practice that prevents students from entering into profound reflections about the sociocultural issues that are intimately entwined with L2 learning. For instance, many SLA researchers (Kramsch 2002, 2005; Byrnes 2006) have recently cautioned the field about falling into a servile application of a transactional methodology of language learning where language negotiations simply reinforce the dominant corporate model of social interaction. They advise the profession not to teach to the needs of only negotiating business, tourist transactions, contracts, and economic exchanges—goals that are too limiting for any meaningful L2 learning environment. Byrnes (2006, 242) warns of the dangers originating from the present communicative classroom where transactional exchanges tend "to perpetuate self-referential notions of the other language and culture." In other words, students learning in this most basic transactional framework end up thinking that other cultures simply carry on their lives in exactly the same way by merely using a different language—a conclusion that ignores all the relevant sociocultural dimensions of the L2 culture and the profound differences with the students' L1 culture.

Accordingly, teachers must put the same kind of thought into using technology in service of the curriculum that they regularly do in selecting specific L2 readings or preparing in-class discussions and other such classroom activities. Using new technology will not make up for lack of planning or foresight but rather will tend to intensify existing classroom methodological deficiencies. Moreover, teachers need to plot out how the introduction of a given technological tool and accompanying tasks will empower students to take control of their own learning process and, consequently, stimulate a more student-centered classroom.

Student-centered Classroom

The idea of a student-centered classroom remains an elusive if not threatening goal for most language teachers, and with good reason. Most teachers were trained in a tradition that puts them at center stage, as the sole providers of authentic, comprehensible input. Krashen's model (see chapter 1) might also be said to reinforce this sense of the teacher-centered classroom because of the emphasis on the teacher's providing students with comprehensible input. Abandoning that time-honored role seems strange and unnatural. More important, the student-centered classroom predictably blurs the traditional roles of authority and expertise (Warschauer, Turbee, and Roberts 1996)—and, for most teachers, that's a disturbing feeling without some previous experience or guidelines on how to handle it.

Integrating technology properly into the curriculum can accelerate the focus on the student-centered classroom. Wikis, blogs, asynchronous and synchronous chat tend to foster a more egalitarian sense of authorship. As the students look at it, why should any single person's contribution to a wiki, even the teacher's, be more important than anyone else's? In the case of webquests, L2 students might not always reach the same informed conclusions about the L2 culture that the teacher had in mind. This is dangerous ground for most teachers: Aren't teachers supposed to tell the students what is important about the target culture in their role as the resident expert? Relinquishing the compulsion to control the flow of information comes hard to most teachers, but, in the case of using technology, many of today's new tools may actually provide affordances to do just that.

Teachers should redirect their energies away from notions of control toward learning objectives that ensure that the tasks and tools will motivate students to become active participants who engage in reflections about both their own culture and the target one. However, sending L2 students to a chat forum (synchronous or asynchronous) to engage native speakers from abroad without a clear lesson plan or preparations will most likely lead to communication breakdowns that reinforce stereotypes and frustrate everyone involved (for an example of this, see Ware and Kramsch 2005). In reaction to these breakdowns, some teachers are prone to intone the familiar mantra, "Well, technology failed me again today." But more often than not, the teacher failed to plan properly; using technology never obviates the need for lesson planning and careful technical preparation, especially if the goal is to involve students as willing and active participants in the process.

Interactivity, Agency, and the Student as Producer

Selber (2004, 24–26)—whose principal interests lie in teaching English composition but whose observations are equally valid for L2 language study—argues that students need to develop three types of computer literacy: (a) functional, using the computer as tool; (b) critical, viewing computer functions as cultural artifacts that imply social dynamics, conventions, and cultures of practice/use that need to be analyzed; and (c) rhetorical, reflecting and then producing new computer-mediated (hyper)texts. This model closely parallels Kern and Warschauer's (2000) view of CALL development (see chapter 3) as having moved away from structural and communicative to more integrative concerns. Clearly teachers and students alike must have a firm grounding in how the tools work (i.e., functional literacy), but a successful incorporation of technology into the language curriculum demands that students reflect on what they are doing (i.e., critical literacy) and then put it into practice (i.e., rhetorical literacy). Students must be guided into probing and analyzing, from both an L1 and an L2 perspective, the cultural values and historical contexts that are embedded in language, computer use, the Internet, chat exchanges, blog entries, web pages, and multimedia. In short, sociocultural research maintains that all things human are embedded in a social context.

As part of the path to reaching critical literacy, Selber (2004, 95–103) suggests that teachers might provide their students with a set of analytical or problem-solving strategies, known in classical rhetoric as heuristics, that can aid students in formulating possible responses to a website activity, a chat exchange, a blog entry, an authentic hypertext with images, or any new set of cultural values or expressions.

Interestingly enough, new technologies have engendered innovative forms of expression that challenge traditional notions of authorship and standard genres. For instance, chat exchanges are blurring the distinctions between oral and written genres. Students, then, are charged with not just negotiating meaning in L2 but also trying to make sense of their world with the inclusion of new L2 elements and forms of expression.

Selber's next required step toward realizing a rhetorical literacy is much bolder: he asks students to produce their own hypertexts so as to become multimedia authors in their own right, "designers of information environments that span time as well as space" (2004, 138). Blogs and wikis come readily to mind. Selber expects a rhetorically literate student to be able to engage with others (or with other materials) in acts of deliberation, reflection, persuasion, and social actions. As discussed in chapter 2, Laurillard (2002, 23) also considers the goal of teaching to be fundamentally a rhetorical one:

"seeking to persuade students to change the way they experience the world through an understanding of the insights of others." Teachers need to help guide their students during this process of change so that they can successfully find their own third place as an evolving bilingual.

The Third Place: Intercultural Communicative Competence (ICC)

Chapter 4 discussed how Kramsch (1993, 2000) and Byram (1997) have championed the idea that students must find their own voice as incipient bilinguals, what Kramsch (1993) has called a third place that combines both their L1 and L2 experiences and knowledge. In essence, Laurillard (2002, 21–22) is referring to this same basic idea when she talks about the mediating role that language plays, especially with reference to academic as opposed to direct experiential learning. Consider figure 6.1.

The ideal learning pathway from many teachers' point of view would have students experience and interpret L2 culture directly through the L2 language without interference from the L1, harkening back to an old behaviorist tenet, "speak only in the target language in class!" In fact, this is exceedingly unhelpful for beginning, intermediate, or even some advanced students and does not appear to be a reasonable path for integrating past experiences with new ones (as those who work in bilingual education programs can readily attest to; Cook 2001). The L1 language and especially the L1 culture unavoidably constitute the student's principal warp and woof for interpreting, conjecturing about, evaluating, and judging all new experiences—even more so with respect to gaining academic knowledge about the L2, its native speakers, and L2 culture. In figure 6.1, this process is represented by the heavy arrow that proceeds from the individual (i.e., EGO) to L2 cultural knowledge. As time goes by, students will consolidate their knowledge of L2 and become more proficient, enjoying a more direct pathway to the L2 culture (the lighter arrow). Yet in constantly defining a third place, no one is entirely free from the effects of previous experiences, especially those that are as deeply engrained as L1 language and culture.

If teachers and/or students ignore this mediation dynamic in constructing the L2 learning environment, the goal of reaching a more profound understanding of ICC becomes all the more difficult. Not surprisingly, the

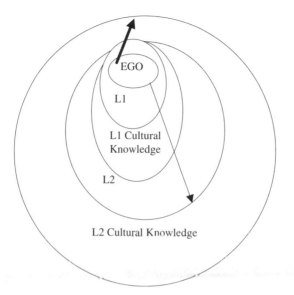

Figure 6.1   The Individual's L2 Learning as Mediated by L1 Language and Culture

process of arriving at that third place will probably end up having the most significant or, at the very least, the most life altering consequences for students who attempt to learn another language. Long after finishing formal language study, our students will remember their intensely personal insights gained about L2 culture, while quite naturally allowing the details of the pluperfect subjunctive forms to lapse into oblivion. This is as it should be, if language teachers stop for a moment to contemplate the nature and value of academic learning.

Striving for a third place, then, is not only a goal for a more internationally oriented curriculum but also a principal objective for those students who will never travel abroad, which is 97 percent our students (Davidson 2007). Because of the changing U.S. demographics, increased diversity at home has heightened the importance of promoting learning languages as part of the core curriculum from a need to embrace our nation's own multiculturalism, quite apart from increasing one's attractiveness to the corporate world that is seeking to hire multilingual employees. Cummins and Sayers (1995, 109) argue for a FL classroom that relies on collaborative critical inquiry, which will, in turn, "promote pride in students' cultural identities and respect for other cultural realities." Technology can facilitate the process of this collaborative critical inquiry if teachers are aware of these goals.

AN EXEMPLAR OF GOOD PRACTICE:
THE CULTURA PROJECT

I return, again, to the goals of the Cultura project (see chapter 4) as an embodiment of this sense of a rhetorical praxis, as well as a realization of Cummins and Sayers's (1995) plea for incorporating global networks into the learning environment. It is not that the technology used in Cultura has become so transparent or sophisticated but rather that the tools are used in conjunction with lesson plans that make students from both countries work toward a new sense of intercultural competence. Notice that I did not say that students will "achieve true understanding" or "come to like or appreciate the target culture." That may or may not happen. Each student must find his or her own third place, a process that surely will involve tension and conflict. But only this type of dialogic approach stands any chance of imparting meaningful intercultural competence as part of the L2 process.

By design, the technology used in the Cultura project is limited to online survey materials, web postings on a bulletin board, and asynchronous e-mail listserv communication. The creators (Furstenberg et al. 2001) eschew synchronous chat on purpose to force the participants to spend time reflecting on and analyzing what they are going to say before they write it. This strategy lowers the emotional stakes, eliminates direct confrontations, and stimulates a willingness to carefully listen to the opinions of the other and, then, enter into reflections. There is nothing dogmatic or magical about these choices; another teacher could adapt the Cultura curriculum so that synchronous chat would make perfect sense, given local circumstances.

The Cultura curriculum further stipulates that each L2 population—whether French L1 speakers or English L1 speakers in the case reported by Furstenberg and colleagues (2001)—expresses their theories and opinions in their respective native languages. In theory, no single group holds a linguistic advantage over another. These L1 thoughts become fodder (i.e., authentic texts) for linguistic analysis in each of the respective L2 classrooms that are conducted in the L2.

The Cultura project is much less about technology and much more about curricular design. The tools provide the right learning environment to allow the teachers and students to accomplish the stated goals, following Hubbard's (2006) advice to take into account both the student fit and teacher fit (see chapter 3). It should be remembered as well that the Cultura curriculum is used minimally with intermediate students. I imagine efforts to apply this approach with beginners would be too frustrating, if not outright counterproductive; considerations of level are also part of finding the right fit.

TOWARD A RHETORICALLY BASED
DIGITAL CLASSROOM

In the last section, I reviewed the common threads that underlie the preceding chapters and general ideas about using technology in the FL curriculum. In this section I outline a specific pedagogy for a rhetorically based digital classroom with particular attention to Laurillard's work (2002).

With respect to higher education, Laurillard (2002, 21) carefully distinguishes between first-order or direct experiential learning—such as what happens in the course of acquiring L1 from birth—and second-order or academic learning, which is necessarily mediated in SLA development by the L1, by L1 culture, and, in the present case, by the use of the computer. Accordingly, academic knowledge relies on symbolic representations, a fact that has drawn considerable attention with respect to mathematical education but has been taken relatively for granted by practitioners in the language field (22). Laurillard (2002, 21) explains that academic knowledge comes about through exposition, argument, interpretation, and reflection—a process very close to Selber's (2004) notion of rhetorical literacy, Cummins and Sayers's (1995) process of collaborative critical inquiry, or Kramsch's (1993) quest for a third place. Consequently, the act/art of teaching consists in helping students go beyond their first-order experiences to change the way they experience the world. That is why teachers can be said to be engaged in a rhetoric practice, the art of influencing the thought and conduct of an audience.

Laurillard (2002, 20) captures this epistemological difference by contrasting the terms *percept*, a result of direct experiential learning (i.e., perceptions), with *precept*, the product of artificial or formal learning environments. The real challenge that teachers face every day in the classroom is how to impart decontextualized knowledge, precepts about L2 language and culture, given that most students will not experience in a direct way by living in the target society but rather only in an academic setting. Her solution is to propose using an iterative conversational framework that first reveals and then takes into account what teachers and students alike bring to the learning environment (e.g., their respective theories, ideas, conceptions, observations; 2002, 87). In processing the variation that exists between them, teachers must also imagine themselves as the learner, which will determine the focus of further dialogue and classroom activities (71). As a consequence of this iterative process, there can never to be said to exist one way of teaching something. Teachers may start out following certain rhetorical heuristics, as mentioned earlier, but the formulation of specific lesson plans must be based on this dialogic process, which in turn depends on the variation of student responses (Marton and Booth 1997, 179).

Herein lies one of the reasons that teachers might resist creating a student-centered learning environment and/or introducing technological assistance: The lesson plans have to be constantly reviewed and adapted based on student reception. Teaching in this fashion, with or without technology, becomes a discovery process, not a deductive exercise in hypothesis testing. Laurillard (2002, 69 and 86–87) calls this discovery process a phenomenographic teaching strategy because it asks teachers to qualitatively assess and then incorporate the variation in students' conceptions into the learning environment, using the following basic pathway:

- Present the learner with new ways of seeing.
- Focus on a few critical issues and show how they relate.
- Integrate substantive and syntactic structures.
- Make the learner's conception explicit to them.
- Highlight the inconsistencies within and the consequences of the learner's conceptions.
- Create situations where learners center attention on relevant aspects.

At all points in the process, teachers must gauge student reaction. Of course, it would be easier to ignore all of this and just give a lecture or play the role of the principal provider of comprehensible input. A pedagogy based on the inspirational lecture or class performance, however, is inherently flawed, as Laurillard explains (2002, 93): "Academics will always defend the value of the *inspirational* lecture, as though this could clinch the argument. But how many inspirational lectures could you reasonably give in a week? How many could a student reasonably absorb? Inspirational lectures are likely to be occasional events. Academics [in their role] as *students* typically think little of the method. It is commonplace to observe that the only valuable parts of an academic conference are the informal sessions."

As part of the conversational framework, Laurillard uses the following twelve-step evaluation checklist to review the affordances that an assortment of educational media may provide: lectures, print, television, video, DVD, hypermedia, enhanced hypermedia, web resources, interactive television, simulations, virtual environments, tutorial programs, games, digital document discussion environments, audio conferencing, videoconferencing, microworlds, collaborative microworlds, and modeling (i.e., creating new software).

1. Teacher can describe conception.
2. Student can describe conception.
3. Teacher can redescribe in light of student's conception or action.
4. Student can redescribe in light of teacher's conception or action.
5. Teacher can adapt task goal in light of student's description or action.
6. Teacher can set task goal.
7. Student can act to achieve task goal.
8. Teacher can set up world to give intrinsic feedback on actions.
9. Student can modify action in light of feedback given.
10. Student can adapt actions in light of teacher's description or student's redescription.
11. Student can reflect on interaction so as to modify redescription.
12. Teacher can reflect on student's action to modify redescription.

Notice that the conversational framework heightens, rather than lessens, the active intervention of teachers, although not necessarily in the role of doing all of the talking. Educational media, depending on their respective affordances, contribute to at least some of the twelve steps of the conversational framework. Print, TV, video, and DVDs provide students with narratives; DVDs and web resources offer students an interactive space; CMC tools assist communications; simulations and iCALL make available an adaptive environment; and, finally, modeling allow students to become productive agents in their own right. An intelligent language curriculum uses a variety of educational media in ways that enable and activate as many steps of the iterative conversational pedagogy as possible.

TEACHING PIGS HOW TO FLY: DEFINING THE LIMITS OF TECHNOLOGY

On the one hand, it should be abundantly clear now that not all technology satisfies all of the goals of the ideal classroom pedagogy, digitally enhanced or otherwise. But no matter: the parts can and do add up to a whole, if carefully thought out in advance. On the other hand, using technology in place of what people do best is tantamount to trying to make pigs fly. And what people do best is carry on dialogues. Using technology to help people carry out conversational exchanges, then, is a good fit. Because academic knowledge is a "consensual description of experience" (Laurillard 2002, 177), the role of teachers who use technology in the curriculum becomes even more important than ever, but perhaps not as the principal protagonist, as is the case in the more traditional teacher-centered classroom.

Accordingly, in this book, discussion and dialogue are the linchpin, the glue of the language learning process that will remain labor intensive despite any and all exemplary uses of technological tools and the persistent administrative pressure to increase productivity (i.e., maintain high student/instructor ratios) through the use of new technologies. Technology, however, does not supplant the teacher (chapter 1, myth 4)—quite the opposite—but its use does impose the requirement that teachers learn how to find the best fit in a way that precludes doing business as usual. The tool by itself cannot be carrying on a dialogue, but teachers can learn a new, more student-centered, more computer rhetorically literate way of present-ing the curriculum where new technologies can help feed the dialogic pro-cess. How can teachers learn to do this?

Fortunately, teachers now have recourse to many online language jour-nals dedicated to providing guidance and the latest research about using technology in service of the language curriculum.[1] These resources exist to stimulate and guide teachers to incorporate technology into the curriculum, but again, teachers have to want to do it.

Likewise, the CALL field now exhibits a marked desire to discuss issues of teacher training in the use of technology in service of the L2 curriculum, as evidenced by the recent spate of publications: for example, Beatty (2003); Colpaert (2006); Donaldson and Haggstrom (2006); Egbert (2005); Egbert, Paulus, and Nakamichi (2002); Felix (2003); Hubbard and Levy (2006b); Kassen et al. (2007); Lai and Zhao (2005); Lomicka and Cooke Plagwitz (2004); and Hauck and Stickler (2006). Kassen et al. (2007, ix) point out that concerns dealing with teacher training and technology fall into five broad categories: national frameworks (e.g., standards, European Common Framework of Reference for Languages, No Child Left Behind), specific contexts (e.g., retraining faculty to teach in e-learning environments, grad-uate student training), e-communities or communities of practice,[2] tool-boxes, and critical reflections. Hubbard and Levy (2006a, 11) define four possible roles for teachers with respect to CALL: practitioner, developer, re-searcher, and trainer. While teachers are minimally asked to perform in the classroom as practitioners, they should aspire to assume other roles as well. Hubbard (2004) also counsels teachers to experience CALL themselves so that they can better understand the students' challenges and frustrations.

Egbert, Paulus, and Nakamichi (2002, 110) observe that language teachers frequently incorporate into the curriculum only those technologies that they use outside of the school environment in their personal lives, despite whatever preservice and in-service training course they have received on CALL. The tendency is to use new technologies to fit current practice rather than trans-forming practice through the application of a new technology (Egbert, Paulus, and Nakamichi 2002, 111). Lam's (2000) study shows that teachers' decisions regarding technology depend crucially on whether the teacher was *personally* convinced of the benefits of using technology for L2 instruction. Given the rapid pace of change in the CALL field (see chapter 1, myth 3), teachers will have to accept that much of their training and retraining will have to come from self-directed learning (Robb 2006). By any measure, then, the key factor for enacting the *Brave New Digital Classroom* still remains each teacher's will to change toward a more student-centered approach that incorporates CALL.

Ironically, constant change is exactly what we are asking our students to do when they step into the language classroom: transform themselves by learning an L2 and finding a new third place vis-à-vis both the L1 and L2. If our best and most experienced language teachers are afraid to harness the power of new technologies or only do so with half-hearted and uninformed attempts (i.e., the "technology failed me again today" syndrome), their students cannot be expected to rise to the challenge of becoming bilingual.

Without a doubt, technology will continue to seep into all facets of our society, including the educational sector (Crystal 2001). The new language classroom will most likely be digitally enhanced, along with the entire educational curriculum at all levels. Continuing education and e-learning will gain more and more prominence as well. Teachers will still be needed to help students make sense of an increasingly multilingual/multicultural world within a progressively more digital learning environment. In this context, training new professionals and retraining seasoned educators in order to enter the *Brave New Digital Classroom* is the responsibility of the field as a whole, but it begins with each teacher's desire to participate in the process of changing how they and their students view the world.

DISCUSSION QUESTIONS AND ACTIVITIES

1.   Explain to a colleague or student what "multiple entry points for using technology" means in terms of teaching or learning a foreign language.

2.   Under what conditions does using a CALL exercise of the drill-and-kill type make sense?

3.   What do researchers mean when they say that culture is mediated by language? What repercussions does this statement have for L2 teaching and learning?

4.   Conduct a survey of your colleagues and/or students: How many of them have reached (a) functional computer literacy, (b) critical computer literacy, or (c) rhetorical computer literacy? What implications do the survey results have for designing your curriculum? What impact would your survey results have on preservice or in-service training?

5.   Review Laurillard's twelve-step checklist for creating a conversational framework for using technology, then examine a single use of technology in your curriculum (e.g., a webquest, a CALL exercise, a CD-ROM activity, a wiki assignment, a CMC task). How many of these steps are implied by this use of technology? Share your results with your colleagues.

6.   What are the similarities and differences between creating a classroom activity that is enhanced with technology and one that is not?

NOTES

1.   For example, CALICO Journal (www.calico.org/), Computer Assisted Language Learning (CALL) (www.tandf.co.uk/journals/titles/09588221.asp), Heritage Language Journal (http://heritagelanguages.org/), Language, Learning and Technology (http://llt.msu.edu/), On-CALL: Australasian Journal of Educational Technology (www.ascilite.org.au/ajet.about/about.html), ReCALL (www.eurocall-languages.org/recall/index.html), and South Asia Language Pedagogy and Technology (http://salpat.uchicago.edu/).
2.   Also for teachers, for example, MERLOT: http://merlot.org/.

Appendix to Chapter 5

The following is a statistical explanation of the student outcomes. Results are considered to be statistically significant if there exists less than a 5 percent probability ($p < 0.05$) that the inference is incorrect (i.e., the null hypothesis). If the probability (p) of making a mistake is greater than 5 percent, the results are said not to be significant. There exist many types of tests for significance. Which test is most appropriate depends on the circumstances under which the study was conducted: for example, equal or unequal number of participants, only two groups or multiple groups involved, a priori predictions about group differences or no predictions.

The Tukey Honestly Significant Difference results are displayed in table A.1. This test is most appropriate when the researcher makes no a priori predictions concerning group differences. It constitutes a more demanding test of significance (hence the name Honestly Significant Difference) and yields an accurate picture of which groups differ according to the measure employed, despite the lack of a previous hypothesis. Using this test, then, the different shadings indicate which groups belong together from a statistical point of view (i.e., groups with the same shading exhibit no group differences). Three statistically distinct groups emerge, which confirms the initial visual impression of figure 5.2. (a) a first-year+ group that includes Spanish 1, 2, 3, and, somewhat more weakly, Spanish 4 (i.e., the first quarter of the second year); (b) a second-year+ group consisting of Spanish 5, 6, 7 (although note that quarter 7 is the beginning of the third year); and (b) the heritage speakers group.

The HSD values for the fourth-quarter traditional learner group (SP4) deserve further comment. While from the point of view of the first-quarter students (SP1), the fourth-quarter ones (SP4) were statistically different but there were no differences among the performance of the second-, third-, and fourth-quarter students (SP2, SP3, and SP4). Clearly the fourth-quarter students represent a transition class period during which these L2 students experience a demonstrable jump in linguistic capabilities to the next plateau (i.e., the level gained by fifth-, sixth-, and seventh-quarter students [SP 5, SP 6, SP 7]).

In table A.2, a group-by-group comparison known as a t test of signifi-cance was carried out between first- and second-quarter traditional students and technology-assisted students (both hybrid and distance learners). Each t value can be matched to a probability calculation (p value) that indicates

Table A.1   Tukey Honestly Significant Difference (HSD) Test for Versant for Spanish Scores by Level (quarters)

Quarters	1	2	3	4	5	6	7	HL
1	—	.97	1.0	.43	.00	.00	.00	.00
2		—	1.0	.97	.00	.00	.00	.00
3			—	.71	.00	.00	.00	.00
4				—	.09	.00	.00	.00
5					—	.77	.36	.00
6						—	1.0	.00
7							—	.00

Table A.2   T-test Results Comparing the DL and Classroom Formats

Level (number of quarters)	First-Quarter In-class Learners ($n = 42$)		Second-Quarter In-class Learners ($n = 17$)		Third-Quarter In-class Learners ($n = 50$)	
First-quarter distance learners ($n = 13$)	$t(53) = 1.03$ $p = 0.35$		—	—	—	—
Second-quarter distance learners ($n = 6$)	—	—	$t(21) = 0.96$ $p = 0.35$		—	—
Hybrid 2V ($n = 15$)	—	—	$t(30) = 1.63$ $p = 0.11$		—	—
Hybrid 3V ($n = 4$)	—	—	—	—	$t(52) = 1.00$ $p = 0.32$	

significance or lack of significance. None of the t values obtained significance, which means that there were no significant differences between the traditional students and either the hybrid or distance learners at the same level of seat time. Accordingly, this measure suggests that the hybrid and distance learners did as well as the traditional learners for the first and second quarters.

Glossary

ACMC (asynchronous CMC). Asynchronous computer-mediated communication programs in deferred time allow students to exchange text messages and, sometimes, sound recordings in the format of an electronic bulletin board organized around threads or topics.

affective filter. A term first proposed by Stephen Krashen to refer to the psychological inhibitions that students erect when learning a foreign language.

affordances. This term refers to the advantages and disadvantages that every technological tool provides its users. Some tools predispose users to doing things in a particular way, which could be both positive and negative.

apperception. This is a process whereby someone learns new information by relating it to the previous knowledge base. In terms of learning language, linguists talk about students' needing to realize the gap between where they are now and where they need to go.

ASR (automatic speech recognition). The process of using computers and their programs to render speech signals into words represented through digital data.

authoring tool. A program that allows nonprogrammers to produce sophisticated software quickly and without extensive knowledge of the programming language that makes it possible. Authoring tools usually have certain preset programming routines or templates that are easy to produce but are relatively inflexible in terms of their design.

blended or hybrid format. A blended or hybrid language class mixes a reduced number of classroom sessions with individual work done outside of class and assisted by technology.

browser. A program that interprets HTML code to create a graphics user interface that is visually oriented.

CALI. Computer-assisted language instruction is similar to CALL and refers to stand-alone programs that aid language learning.

CALL. Computer-assisted language learning refers to any software program that aids students in learning another language.

CBI. Content-based instruction for language learning asks students to focus on the subject content first and approaches learning the linguistic features as a by-product of content work.

CD-ROM. Compact Disc Read-Only Memory refers to a medium that holds digital information, games, programs, and music.

CGI scripts. Common gateway interface is a programming protocol used with servers to pass information or requests collected by the server to external applications or other individual users.

chat. This is a form of CMC communication that most often refers to synchronous online communication.

chatterbot program. The chatterbot program provides users with a conversational agent that simulates having artificial intelligence. Most chatterbot programs match key words to a stock set of responses in order to feign interactivity.

CMC (computer-mediated communication). Any program that allows users to exchange language—through text or audio. For instance, e-mail, blogs, wikis, forums, IM, and chat.

CMS/LMS. Course management systems or learning management systems are a suite of authoring tools that allow teachers and students to organize their online e-learning materials, complete with content posting, grade books, and communication tools.

comprehensible input. This term was made popular by Steve Krashen and refers to linguistic input that is just slightly more difficult than the learner is used to but still comprehensible (i.e., $<i+1>$).

DVD. The Digital Video Disc provides large amounts of optical storage of information. DVDs are the same physical dimension as CD-ROMs but with six times the amount of storage capacity.

FonF (focus on form). Focus on form should be contrasted with focus on forms, where the former allows students to discover form differences through meaningful practice while the latter imparts information (i.e., lectures) about the linguistic form differences without contextualized practice.

forums, discussion boards, or electronic bulletin board. This term refers to an online message board where posts are displayed chronologically or in threaded discussions.

FTP. The file transfer protocol is used to transfer files from local areas (a single computer) to a server where files can be made publicly available through the Internet.

GUI. A graphics user interface turns machine code into a visual metaphor that can be modified and manipulated.

hosting. Programs that are accessible on the Internet must be publicly published on a server connected to the World Wide Web. Someone or some institution must offer hosting on a server for their users where they can store their programs.

HTML. Hypertext markup language is the programming language that browsers can interpret in order to create web pages with a graphics interface.

HTTP. Hypertext transfer protocol is the programming convention used for publishing pages on the Internet.

iCALL. Intelligent computer-assisted language learning refers to programs that exhibit a modicum of artificial intelligence, the ability to respond to users' needs and demands.

ICC (intercultural communicative competence). As a counterpoint to Chomsky's notion of linguistic competence, ICC refers to knowledge of another people's culture as mediated through language.

ILR rating scale. The Interagency Language Roundtable scale is a set of descriptions of abilities to communicate in a language. It was originally developed by the United States Foreign Service Institute, the predecessor of the National Foreign Affairs Training Center. Thus it is also often called Foreign Service Levels. It consists of descriptions of five levels of language proficiency.

interlanguage. When people learn a second language, the developing internal grammar, albeit incomplete, is referred to as their interlanguage.

Internet. The Internet is a worldwide, publicly accessible network of interconnected computers that transmit data by packet switching using the standard Internet protocol (IP). It includes millions of smaller domestic, academic, business, and government networks.

JavaScript. This programming language can be used in conjunction with HTML code to enhance a web page's interactivity.

LAD. The language acquisition device, the innate capacity to construct a grammar.

link rot. When the address of a web page is no longer operative.

MOO. A MUD (multiuser domain) Object Oriented is a type of domain that allows users to connect to each other via the computer and share a virtual reality.

PERL (practical extraction and reporting language). A dynamic programming language that is used to create highly interactive programs and web pages.

SCMC (synchronous CMC). Refers to chat in real time that includes the exchange of text, audio, and/or video.

tandem language learning. This term refers to the pairing up of two speakers of different languages so that each one can teach the other his or her native language.

telnet. The telecommunication network is a protocol used to allow users to communicate with each other over the Internet. It was originally developed for the UNIX operating system.

Unicode. Unicode is a standardized protocol that permits computers to represent the text of any language in a constant way. Only Unicode-compliant programs allow users to type in non-Romance languages such as Chinese, Arabic, or Korean.

URL. The uniform resource locator is the address for a web page that follows the HTTP protocol.

VoIP. A program that implements voice over internet protocol or Internet telephony allows users to speak to one another via computer as if they were using a telephone.

webquest. This is an educational research activity where students use the web to investigate and analyze assigned topics.

world English. People from around the world speak English but not in the same way that native speakers from America or England do.

WWW (World Wide Web). A system of interlinked hypertext documents available through the Internet.

WYSIWYG. What You See Is What You Get refers to a system that makes the content editing appear identical to the final visual product.

References

Abrams, Z. I. 2003. The effects of synchronous and asynchronous CMC on oral performance. *Modern Language Journal* 87(2): 157–67.

———. 2006. From theory to practice: Intracultural CMC in the L2 classroom. In *Calling on CALL: From theory and research to new directions in foreign language teaching*, ed. L. Ducate and N. Arnold, 181–209. CALICO Monograph Series, vol. 5. San Marcos, TX: CALICO.

ACTFL. 1996. *Standards for foreign language learning: Executive Summary*. Retrieved August 31, 2007, from www.actfl.org/i4a/pages/index.cfm?pageid=3324.

Adair-Hauck, B., L. Willingham-McLain, and B. Earnest-Youngs. 1999. Evaluating the integration of technology and second language learning. *CALICO Journal* 17(2): 269–306.

Al-Batal, M. 2007. Arabic and national language educational policy. *Modern Language Journal* 91(2): 268–71.

Allen, I. E., and J. Seaman. 2006. *Making the grade: Online education in the United States, 2006*. Needham, MA: Sloan Consortium. Retrieved January 11, 2007, from www.sloan-c.org/publications/survey/index.asp.

———. 2007. Online nation: Five years of growth in online learning. Needham, MA: Sloan Consortium. Retrieved April 2, 2008, from www.sloan-c.org/publications/survey/pdf/online-nation/pdf.

Arnold, N., and L. Ducate. 2006. CALL: Where are we and where do we go from here? In *Calling on CALL: From theory and research to new directions in foreign language teaching*, ed. N. Arnold and L. Ducate, 1–20. CALICO Monograph Series, vol. 5. San Marcos, TX: CALICO.

Arocena, F. 2006. *Webmaestro*. Retrieved March 27, 2006, from www.axis.org/usuarios/farocena/.

Arvan, L., and D. Musumeci. 1999. Instructor attitudes within the SCALE efficiency projects. Retrieved July 14, 2006, from www.sloanc.org/conference/proceedings/1999Summer/papers/99summer_arvan.pdf.

Bañados, E. 2006. A blended-learning pedagogical model for teaching and learning EFL successfully through an online interactive multimedia environment. *CALICO Journal* 23(3): 533–50.

Barson, J. 1991. The virtual classroom is born: What now? In *Foreign language acquisition research and the classroom*, ed. B. F. Freed, 364–83. Lexington, MA: Heath and Company.

Bauer, B., L. deBenedette, G. Furstenberg, S. Levet, and S. Waryn. 2006. The Cultura project. In *Internet-mediated intercultural foreign language education*, ed. J. A. Belz and S. L. Thore, 31–62. Boston: Thomson Heinle.

Beatty, K. 2003. *Teaching and researching computer-assisted language learning*. London: Longman.

Belz, J. A. 2002. Social dimensions of telecollaborative foreign language study. *Language Learning & Technology* 6(1): 60–81. Retrieved December 10, 2006, from http://llt.msu.edu/vol6num1/belz/.

———. 2003. Linguistic perspectives on the development of intercultural competence in telecollaboration. *Language Learning & Technology* 7(2): 68–117. Retrieved July 18, 2006, from http://llt.msu.edu/vol7num2/belz.

Belz, J. A., and S. L. Thorne, eds. 2006. *Internet-mediated intercultural foreign language education.* Boston: Thomson Heinle.

Bernstein, J., I. Barbier, E. Rosenfeld, and J. De Jong. 2004. Development and validation of an automatic spoken Spanish test. In InSTIL/ICALL 2004 symposium on computer assisted learning, NLP and speech technologies in advanced language learning systems, Venice, Italy, June 17–19, 2004, ISCA Archive. Retrieved May 2, 2006, from www.isca-speech.org/archive/icall2004.

Bertin, J.-C. 2001. CALL material structure and learner competence. In *ICT and language learning: A European perspective*, ed. A. Chambers and G. Davies, 83–100.

Bialystok, E., and K. Hakuta. 1994. *In other words.* New York: Basic Books.

Bickerton, D., T. Stenton, and M. Temmerman. 2001. In *ICT and language learning: A European perspective*, ed. A. Chambers and G. Davies, 53–66. Lisse: Sets and Zeitlinger.

Blake, R. 2000. Computer-mediated communication: A window on L2 Spanish interlanguage. *Language Learning & Technology* 4(1): 120–36.

———. 2005a. Bimodal chatting: The glue of a distance language learning course. *CALICO Journal* 22(3): 497–511.

———. 2005b. Review of Wimba: Voice management system 4.0. Ed. Jack Burston. Digital Language Lab Solutions. IALLT. 54–66.

———. 2006. Two heads are better than one: C[omputer] M[ediated] C[ommunication] for the L2 Curriculum. In *Changing language education through CALL*, ed. R. P. Donaldson and M. A. Haggstrom, 229–48. Abingdon: Routledge.

———. 2008. New trends in using technology in the language curriculum. *2007 Annual Review of Applied Linguistics* 27 (March): 76–97.

Blake, R., J. Blasco, and C. Hernández. 2001. *Tesoros* CD-ROM: *A multi-media-based course.* Boecillo, Valladolid: Boecillo Editorial Multimedia (BeM) and New York: McGraw-Hill.

Blake, R., and A. Delforge. 2005. Language learning at a distance: Spanish without walls. In *Selected papers from the 2004 NFLRC symposium: Distance education, distributed learning and language instruction (NetWork#44)* [IITML document], ed. I. Thompson and D. Hiple. Honolulu: University of Hawai'i, National Foreign Language Resource Center. Retrieved June 16, 2006, from http://nflrc.hawaii.edu/NetWorks/NW44.

Blake, R., M. V. González Pagani, A. Ramos, and M. Marks. 2003. *Al corriente: Curso intermedio de español.* New York: McGraw-Hill.

Blake, R., and C. Kramsch. 2007. Introduction to perspective volume. *Modern Language Journal* 91(2): 247–49.

Blake, R., and E. Zyzik. 2003. Who's helping whom? Learner/heritage speakers' networked discussions in Spanish. *Applied Linguistics* 24(4): 519–44.

Bley-Vroman, R. 1990. The logical problem of foreign language learning. *Linguistic Analysis* 20(1–2): 3–49.

Blyth, C. S. 1999. *Untangling the web: Nonce's guide to language and culture on the Internet.* New York: Nounce Publishing Consultants.

Brandl, K. 2002. Integrating internet-based reading materials into the foreign language curriculum: From teacher- to student-centered approaches. *Language Learning & Technology* 6(3): 87–107. Retrieved June 8, 2006, from http://llt.msu.edu/vol6num3/brandl/default.html.

———. 2005. Are you ready to *MOODLE? Language Learning and Technology* 9(2): 16–23. Retrieved June 12, 2006, from http://llt.msu.edu/vol9num2/review1/default.html.

Brecht, R., D. Davidson, and R. Ginsberg. 1995. Predictors of foreign language gain during study abroad. In *Second language acquisition in a study abroad context,* ed. Barbara F. Freed, 37–66. Amsterdam: John Benjamin.

Brinton, D., M. A. Snow, and M. Wesche. 1989. *Content-based second language instruction.* Boston: Heinle & Heinle.

Brown, H. D. 2001. *Teaching by principles: An interactive approach to language pedagogy.* White Plains, NY: Addison Wesley Longman.

Bruner, J. 1996. *The culture of education.* Cambridge, MA: Harvard University Press.

Burston, J. 1998. Antidote 98. *CALICO Journal* 16(2): 197–212.

———. 2003. Software selection: A primer on sources and evaluation. *CALICO Journal* 21(1): 29–40.

———. 2006. Working towards effective assessment of CALL. In *Changing language education through CALL,* ed. R. P. Donaldson and M. A. Haggstrom, 249–70. London: Routledge.

Byram, M. 1997. *Teaching and assessing intercultural communicative competence.* Clevedon, UK: Multilingual Matters.

Byram, M., B. Gribkova, and H. Starkey. 2002. *Developing the intercultural dimension in language teaching: A practical introduction for teachers.* Strasborg: Council of Europe.

Byrnes, H. 2000. Languages across the curriculum—Interdepartmental curriculum construction. In *Languages across the curriculum: Interdisciplinary structures and internationalized education,* ed. M-R. Kecht and K. von Hammerstein, 151–75. National East Asian Languages Resource Center. Columbus: Ohio State University.

———. 2006. Perspectives. *Modern Language Journal* 90(2): 244–46.

Cahill, D., and D. Catanzaro. 1997. Teaching first-year Spanish on-line. *CALICO Journal* 14(2): 97–114.

Carnegie Mellon University. 2000. *Elementary French online.* Retrieved December 10, 2006, from http://ml.hss.cmu.edu/languageonline/overview/overview.html.

Carr, S. 2000. As distance education comes of age, the challenge is keeping up with the students. *Chronicle of Higher Education,* p. A3. Retrieved December 10, 2005, from www.chronicle.com.

Chapelle, C. 2001. *Computer applications in second language acquisition: Foundations for teaching, testing, and research.* Cambridge: Cambridge University Press.

————. 2005. CALICO at center stage: Our emerging rights and responsibilities. *CALICO Journal* 23(1): 5–15.

Chen, Chin-chi. 2006. How webquests send technology to the background. In *Teacher education in CALL,* ed. P. Hubbard and M. Levy, 221–34. Language Learning & Language Teaching Series, vol. 14. Philadelphia: John Benjamin.

Chenoweth, N. A., C. M. Jones, and G. R. Tucker. 2006. Language online: Principles of design and methods of assessment. In *Changing language education through CALL,* ed. R. P. Donaldson and M. A. Haggstrom, 146–67. Abingdon: Routledge.

Chenoweth, N. A., and K. Murday. 2003. Measuring student learning in an online French course. *CALICO Journal* 20(2): 284–314.

Chomsky, N. 1986. *Knowledge of language: Its nature, origin, and use.* New York: Praeger.

Chun, D. 1994. Using computer networking to facilitate the acquisition of interactive competence. *System* 22(1): 17–31.

————. 1998. Using computer-assisted class discussion to facilitate the acquisition of interactive competence. In. *Language learning online: Theory and practice in the ESL and L2 computer classroom,* ed. J. Swaffar, S. Romano, P. Markley, and K. Arens, 57–80. Austin, TX: Labyrinth.

————. 2006. CALL technologies for L2 reading. In *Calling on CALL: From theory and research to new directions in foreign language teaching,* ed. L. Ducate and N. Arnold, 81–98. CALICO Monograph Series, vol. 5. San Marcos, TX: CALICO.

Chun, D. M. and J. L. Plass. 1997. Research on text comprehension in multimedia environment. *Language Learning & Technology* 1(1): 60–81.

Clifford, R. 1987. The status of computer-assisted language learning. *CALICO Journal* 4(4): 9–16.

Cohen, A., and J. Sykes. 2006. *Dancing with words: Strategies for learning pragmatics in Spanish.* Retrieved May 11, 2006, from www.carla.umn.edu/speechacts/sp_pragmatics/home.html.

Colpaert. J. 2006. Pedagogy-driven design for online language teaching and learning. *CALICO Journal* 23(3): 477–97.

Cook, V. J. 2001. Using the first language in the classroom. *Canadian Modern Language Review* 57(3): 402–23.

Crandall, J., and G. R. Tucker. 1990. Content-based instruction in second and foreign languages. In *Foreign language education: Issues and strategies,* ed. A. Padilla, H., Fairchild, and C. Valadez, 187–200. Newbury Park, CA: Sage.

Crump, B., and A. McIlroy. 2003. The digital divide: Why the "don't–want–tos" won't compute: Lessons from a New Zealand ICT project. *First Monday* 8(12). Retrieved June 27, 2006, from http://firstmonday.org/issues/issue8_12/crump/index.html.

Crystal, D. 2001. *Language and the Internet.* Cambridge: Cambridge University Press.

Cummins, J. 1998. E-Lective language learning: Design of a computer-assisted text-based ESL/EFL learning system. *TESOL Journal* 7(3): 18–21.

Cummins, J., and D. Sayers. 1995. *Brave new schools: Challenging cultural literacy through global learning networks*. New York: St. Martin's Press.

Cziko, G. A., and S. Park. 2003. Internet audio communications for second language learning: A comparative view of six programs. *Language Learning & Technology* 7(1): 15–27. Retrieved June 1, 2006, from http://llt.msu.edu/vol7num1/review1/default.html.

Davidson, D. 2004. Capabilities and outputs of the U.S. education system: Proficiency outputs. *The National Language Conference*. Retrieved July 17, 2006, from www.nlconference.org/docs/NLC_Commentary_Davidson.doc.

———. 2007. Study abroad and outcomes measurements: The case of Russian. *Modern Language Journal* 91(2): 276–80.

Davies, G., ed. 2006. *Information and communications technology for language teachers (ICT4LT)*. Slough, Thames Valley University. Retrieved August 31, 2006, from www.ict4lt.org.

Debski, R. 1997. Support of creativity and collaboration in the language classroom: A new role for technology. In *Language learning through social computing: ALAA's occasional papers*, ed. R. Debski, J. Gassin, and M. Smith, 16, 39–65. Melbourne: Applied Linguistics Association of Australia.

DeKeyser, R. M. 2000. The robustness of critical period effects in second language acquisition. *Studies in Second Language Acquisition* 22(4): 499–533.

Delcloque, P. 2001. DISSEMINATE or not? Should we pursue a new direction: Looking for the *third way* in CALL development? In *ICT and language learning: A European perspective*, ed. A. Chambers and G. Davies, 67–82. Lisse: Sets and Zeitlinger.

Dodge, B. 2002. *Webquest taskonomy: A taxonomy of tasks*. Retrieved June 10, 2006, from http://webquest.sdsu.edu/taskonomy.html.

Donaldson, R. P., and M. A. Haggstrom. 2006. *Changing language education through CALL*. Abington: Routledge.

Doughty, C. 1998. Acquiring competence in a second language: Form and function. In *Learning foreign and second languages*, ed. Heidi Byrnes, 128–56. New York: Modern Language Association.

Doughty, C. J., and M. H. Long, eds. 2003a. *The handbook of second language acquisition*. London: Blackwell.

———. 2003b. Optimal psycholinguistic environments for distance foreign language learning. *Language Learning & Technology* 7(3): 50–80. Retrieved March 4, 2006, from http://llt.msu.edu/vol7num3/doughty.

Dubreil, S. 2006. Getting perspective on culture through CALL. In *Calling on CALL: From theory and research to new directions in foreign language teaching*, ed. L. Ducate and N. Arnold, 237–68. CALICO Monograph Series, vol. 5. San Marcos, TX: CALICO.

Ducate, L., and L. Lomicka. 2005. Exploring the blogosphere: Use of web logs in the foreign language classroom. *Foreign Language Annals* 38(3): 408–19.

Echávez-Solano, N. 2003. A comparison of student outcomes and attitudes in technology-enhanced vs. traditional second-semester Spanish language courses. Unpublished PhD diss., University of Minnesota, Minneapolis.

Egbert, J. 2005. *CALL essentials: Principles and practice in CALL classrooms.* Alexandria, VA: TESOL.

Egbert, J., T. Paulus, and Y. Nakamichi. 2002. The impact of CALL instruction on classroom computer use: A foundation for rethinking technology in teacher education. *Language Learning & Technology* 6(3): 106–26. Retrieved June 25, 2007, from http://llt.msu.edu/vol6num3/egbert/default.html.

Ehsani, F., and E. Knodt. 1998. Speech technology in computer-aided language learning: Strengths and limitations of a new CALL paradigm. *Language Learning & Technology* 2(1): 54–73. Retrieved January 1, 2007, from http://llt.msu.edu/vol2num1/article3/.

Ellis, N. C. 2002. Frequency effects in language processing: A review with implications for theories of implicit and explicit language acquisition. *Studies in Second Language Acquisition* 24(2): 143–88.

Ellis, R. 1994. *A study of second language acquisition.* Oxford: Oxford University Press.

———. 1997. *Second language acquisition.* Oxford: Oxford University Press.

———. 2003. *Task-based language teaching and learning.* Oxford: Oxford University Press.

Epps, M. 2004. CALL: How does it make you feel? Unpublished master's thesis, University of Virginia, Charlottesville.

Eskenazi, M. 1999. Using automatic speech processing for foreign language pronunciation tutoring: Some issues and a prototype. *Language Learning & Technology* 2(2): 62–76. Retrieved January 2, 2007, from http://llt.msu.edu/vol2num2/article3/.

Eskenazi, M., and J. Brown. 2006. Teaching the creation of software that uses speech recognition. In *Teacher education in CALL,* ed. P. Hubbard and M. Levy, 135–51. Language Learning & Language Teaching Series, vol. 14. Philadelphia: John Benjamin.

Federal Language Training Laboratory. 1990. *Éxito: High Technology Teaching Basic Spanish.* Washington, DC.

Felix, U. 2003. Teaching language online: Deconstructing the myths. *Australasian Journal of Educational Technology* 19(1): 118–38.

Fidelman, C. 1995–96. A language professional's guide to the world wide web. *CALICO Journal* 13(2–3): 113–40.

Fleming, S., D. Hiple, and Y. Du. 2002. Foreign language distance education: The University of Hawai'i experience. In *New technologies and language learning: Cases in the less commonly taught languages,* ed. C. A. Spreen, 13–54. Technical Report no. 25. Honolulu, HI: Second Language Teaching & Curriculum Center.

Fogg, B. J. 2003. *Persuasive technology: Using computers to change what we think and do.* Amsterdam: Morgan Kaufmann.

Freinet, C. 1994. *Les oeuvres pédagogiques.* Paris: Edition Seuil.

Fryer, L., and R. Carpenter. 2006. Emerging technologies: Bots as language learning tools. *Language Learning & Technology* 10(3): 8–14.

Fukkink, R. G., J. Hulstijn, and A. Simis. 2005. Does training of second-language word recognition skills affect reading comprehension? An experimental study. *Modern Language Journal* 89(1): 54–75.

Furstenberg, G., S. Levet, K. English, and K. Maillet. 2001. Giving a virtual voice to the silent language of culture: The *Cultura* project. *Language Learning & Technology* 5(1): 55–102. Retrieved July 13, 2006, from http://llt.msu.edu/vol5num1/furstenberg/default.html.

Gale, L. E. 1989. *Macario, Montevidisco,* and *Interactive Dígame*: Developing interactive video for language instruction. In *Modern technology in foreign language education: Applications and projects,* ed. W. F. Smith, 235–48. Lincolnwood, IL: National Textbook.

Garrett, N., and P. Liddell. 2004. The new language centers: New mandates, new horizons. In *New perspectives on CALL for second language classrooms,* ed. S. Fotos and C. Browne, 27–40. Mahwah, NJ: Lawrence Erlbaum Associates.

Garrett, Nina. 1986. The problem with grammar: What kind can the language learner use? *Modern Language Journal* 70(2): 133–48.

———. 1988. Computers in foreign language education: Teaching, learning, and language-acquisition research. *ADFL Bulletin* 19(3): 6–12. Retrieved June 27, 2006, from http://www.mla.org/adfl/bulletin/V19N3/193006.htm.

———. 1991. Technology in the service of language learning: Trends and issues. *Modern Language Journal* 75(1): 74–101.

Gass, S., and L. Selinker. 2001. Second language acquisition: An introductory course, 2nd ed. Hillsdale, NJ: Lawrence Erlbaum Associates.

Gass, S. M. 1997. *Input, interaction, and the second language learner.* Mahwah, NJ: Lawrence Erlbaum Associates.

Gass, S. M., A. Mackey, and T. Pica. 1998. The role of input and interaction in second language acquisition: Introduction to the special issue. *Modern Language Journal* 82(3): 299–307.

Gass, S. M., and E. Varonis. 1994. Input, interaction and second language production. *Studies in Second Language Acquisition* 16(3): 283–302.

Genesee, F. 1994. Integrating language and content: Lessons from immersion. *Educational Practice Report 11.* National Center for Research on Cultural Diversity and Second Language Learning. Retrieved June 9, 2006, from www.ncbe.gwu.edu/miscpubs/ncrcdsll/epr11.htm.

Global Reach. 2004. Retrieved June 7, 2006, from http://global-reach.biz/globstats/index.php3.

Godwin-Jones, B. 1998. Dynamic web page creation. *Language Learning & Technology,* 1(2): 9–15. Retrieved June 7, 2006, from http://llt.msu.edu/vol1num2/emerging/default.html.

———. 2002. Multilingual computing. *Language Learning & Technology* 6(2): 6–11. Retrieved July 7, 2006, from http://llt.msu.edu/vol6num2/emerging/default.html.

———. 2003a. Emerging technologies: Blogs and wikis: environments for on-line collaboration. *Language Learning & Technology* 7(2): 12–16. Retrieved April 2, 2006, from http://llt.msu.edu/vol7num2/emerging/.

———. 2003b. Emerging technologies: Tools for distance education: Toward convergence and integration. *Language Learning & Technology* 7(3): 18–22. Retrieved September 1, 2006, from http://llt.msu.edu/vol7num3/emerging/.

————. 2004. Language in action: From webquests to virtual realities. *Language Learning & Technology* 8(3): 9–14. Retrieved June 17, 2006, from http://llt.msu.edu/vol8num3/emerging/default.html.

Goertler, S., and P. Winke, eds. 2008. *Opening doors through distance language education: Principles, perspectives, and practices.* San Marcos, TX: CALICO.

Gonglewski, M. 1999. Linking the Internet to the National Standards for Foreign Language Learning. *Foreign Language Annals* 32(3): 348–62.

Goodfellow, R., I. Jeffreys, T. Miles, and T. Shirra. 1996. Face-to-face learning at a distance? A study of a videoconferencing try-out. *ReCALL* 8(2): 5–16.

Grabe, W. 2004. Research on teaching reading. *Annual Review of Applied Linguistics* 24 (March): 44–69.

Green, A., and B. Earnest-Youngs. 2001. Using the web in elementary French and German courses: Quantitative and qualitative study results. *CALICO Journal* 19(1): 89–123.

Grefenstette, J. N. 2000. Estimation of English and non-English language use on the WWW. *Proceedings of RIAO<#213>2000: Content-based multimedia information access.* Paris, April 12–14. 237–46.

Gregg, K. 1984. Krashen's monitor and Occam's razor. *Applied Linguistics* 5(2): 79–100.

Hanson-Smith, E. 2006. Communities of practice for pre- and in-service teacher education. In *Teacher education in CALL*, ed. P. Hubbard and M. Levy, 305–15. Language Learning & Language Teaching Series, vol. 14. Philadelphia: John Benjamin.

Hatch, E. 1978. Acquisition of syntax in a second language. In *Understanding second and foreign language learning: Issues and approaches*, ed. J. Richards, 34–70. Rowley, MA: Newbury House.

Hauck, M., and U. Stickler. 2006. *What does it take to teach online? CALICO Journal* 23(3): 463–75.

Heift, T. 2001. Intelligent language tutoring systems for grammar practice. Zeitschrift für Interkulturellen Fremdsprachenunterricht [online], 6(2): 15. Retrieved December 28, 2006, from www.spz.tu-darmstadt.de/projekt_ejournal/jg-06-2/beitrag/heift2.htm.

————. 2002. Learner control and error correction in ICALL: Browsers, peekers and adamants. *CALICO Journal* 19(3): 295–313.

————. 2004. Corrective feedback and learner uptake in CALL. *ReCALL* 16(2): 416–31.

Heift, T., and M. Schulze. 2007. *Parsers and pedagogues: Errors and intelligence in computer assisted language learning.* London: Routledge.

Holliday, L. 1995. NS syntactic modifications in NS-NSS negotiation as input data for second language acquisition of syntax. Unpublished PhD diss., University of Pennsylvania, Philadelphia.

Holmberg, B., M. Shelley, and C. White. 2005. *Distance education and languages: Evolution and change.* Clevedon: Multilingual Matters.

Horn, R. 1992. How to get little or no effect and make no significant difference. *Performance and instruction*, 31 (January): 29–32. Retrieved July 10, 2006, from http://66.249.93.104/search?q=cache:dpTmrkyUrogJ:www.stanford.edu/~rhorn/

a/topic/edu/artclHowtoGetLttleorNoEffct.pdf+no+significant+differences&hl=
en&gl=es&ct=clnk&cd=6&client=firefox-a.

Hubbard, P. 1996. Elements of CALL methodology: Development, evaluation, and
implementation. In *The power of CALL*, ed. M. Pennington, 15–33. Bolsover, TX:
Athelstan.

———. 2004. Learner training for effective use of CALL. In *New perspectives on
CALL for the second language classroom*, ed. S. Fotos and C. Browne, 45–67. Mahwah, NJ: Lawrence Erlbaum Associates.

———. 2006. Evaluating CALL software. In *Calling on CALL: From theory and research to new directions in foreign language teaching*, ed. L. Ducate and N. Arnold,
313–38. San Marcos, TX: CALICO.

Hubbard, P., and C. Bradin Siskin. 2004. Another look at tutorial CALL. *ReCALL*
16(2): 448–61.

Hubbard, P., and M. Levy. 2006a. The scope of CALL education. In *Teacher education in CALL*, ed. P. Hubbard and M. Levy, 3–20. Philadelphia: John Benjamin.

———, eds. 2006b. *Teacher education in CALL*. Language Learning & Language
Teaching Series, vol. 14. Philadelphia: John Benjamin.

Hymes, D. 1974. *Foundations in sociolinguistics. An ethnographic approach*. Philadelphia. University of Pennsylvania Press.

Internet World Stats. 2006. Retrieved June 3, 2006, from http://www.internet
worldstats.com/stats7.htm.

Jeon-Ellis, G., R. Debski, and J. Wigglesworth. 2005. Oral interaction around computers in the project-oriented CALL classroom. *Language Learning and Technology* 9(3). 121–45. Retrieved June 7, 2006, from http://llt.msu.edu/vol9num3
/jeon/default.html.

Jones, C. M. 1999. Introduction to special issue on language courseware design.
CALICO Journal 17(1): 5–7.

Juozulynas, V. 1994. Errors in the compositions of second-year German students: An
empirical study for parser-based iCALL. *CALICO Journal* 12(1): 5–17.

Karp, A. 2002. Modification of glosses and its effect on incidental L2 vocabulary
learning in Spanish. Unpublished PhD diss., University of California, Davis.

Kassen, M. A., R. Z. Lavine, K. Murphy-Judy, and M. Peters. 2007. *Preparing and developing technology-proficient L2 teachers*. CALICO Monograph Series, vol. 6. San
Marcos, TX: CALICO.

Keeton, M. T. 2004. Best online instructional practices: Report of phase I of an on-
going study. *Journal of Asynchronous Learning Networks* 8(2): 75–100.

Kern, R. 1995. Restructuring classroom interaction with networked computers: Effects on quantity and quality of language production. *Modern Language Journal*
79(4): 457–76.

Kern, R., P. Ware, and M. Warschauer. 2004. Crossing frontiers: New directions in
online pedagogy and research. *Annual Review of Applied Linguistics* 24 (March):
243–60.

Kern, R. G., and M. Warschauer. 2000. Theory and practice of network-based
language teaching. In *Network-based language teaching: Concepts and practice*,

ed. M. Warschauer and R. Kern, 1–19. Cambridge: Cambridge University Press.

Knight, S. 1994. Dictionary use while reading: The effects on comprehension and vocabulary acquisition for students of different verbal abilities. *Modern Language Journal* 78(3): 285–99.

Kramsch, C. 1986. Proficiency versus achievement: Reflections on the proficiency movement. *ADFL Bulletin*, 18, 22–24. Retrieved July 10, 2006, from http://web2 .adfl.org/adfl/bulletin/v18n1/181022.htm.

————. 1993. *Context and culture in language teaching*. Oxford: Oxford University Press.

————. 2000. Social discursive construction of self in L2 learning. In *Sociocultural theory and second language learning*, ed. J. Lantolf, 133–54. Oxford: Oxford University Press.

————. 2002. In search of the intercultural. *Journal of Sociolinguistics* 6(2): 275–85.

————. 2005. Post 9/11: Foreign languages between knowledge and power. *Applied Linguistics* 26(4): 545–67.

Kramsch, C., and R. Anderson. 1999. Teaching text and context through multimedia. *Language Learning & Technology* 2(2): 31–42. Retrieved June 11, 2006, from http://llt.msu.edu/vol2num2/article1/index.html.

Kramsch, C., F. A'Ness, and W. S. E. Lam. 2000. Authenticity and authorship in the computer-mediated acquisition of L2 literacy. *Language Learning & Technology* 4(2): 78–104. Retrieved June 7, 2006, from http://llt.msu.edu/vol4num2/kramsch /default.html.

Krashen, S. 1982. *Principles and practice in second language acquisition*. London: Pergamon.

————. 1985. *The input hypothesis: issues and implications*, London: Longman.

————. 2004. *The power of reading*. Westport, CT: Libraries Unlimited.

Krashen, S., and T. Terrell. 1983. *The natural approach: Language acquisition in the classroom*. Oxford: Pergamon Press.

Lafford, B. 2004. Review of *Tell me more*. *Language learning & technology* 8(3): 21–34. Retrieved January 1, 2007, from http://llt.msu.edu/vol8num3/review1.

Lafford, P., and B. Lafford. 2005. CMC technologies for teaching foreign languages: What's on the horizon? *CALICO Journal* 22(3): 679–710.

Lafford, B., P. Lafford, and J. Sykes. 2007. *Entre dicho y hecho* . . . : An assessment of the application of research from second language acquisition and related fields to the creation of Spanish CALL materials for lexical acquisition. *CALICO Journal* 24(3): 497–529.

Lai, C., and Y. Zhao. 2005. Introduction: The essence of second language education and technology integration. In *Research in technology and second language learning: Developments and Directions*, ed. Y. Zhao, 401–9. Greenwich, CT: Information Age.

Lai, P., and J. Biggs. 1994. Who benefits from mastery learning? *Contemporary Educational Psychology* 19(1): 13–23.

Lam, Y. 2000. Technophilia v. technophobia: A preliminary look at why second language teachers do or do not use technology in their classrooms. *Canadian Modern Language Review* 56(3): 389–420.

Lange, D. L., C. A. Klee, R. M. Paige, and Y. A. Yershova, eds. 2000. *Culture as the core: Interdisciplinary perspectives on culture learning in the language curriculum.* Minneapolis, MN: Center for Advanced Research on Language Acquisition.

Lantolf, J., ed. 2000. *Sociocultural theory and second language learning.* Oxford: Oxford University Press.

Lantolf, J., and W. Frawley. 1988. Proficiency: Understanding the construct. *Studies in Second Language Acquisition* 10(2): 181–95.

Larsen-Freeman, D., and M. Long. 1991. *An introduction to second language acquisition research.* New York: Longman.

Laurillard, D. 2002. *Rethinking university teaching* (2nd ed.). London: Routledge.

Leaver, B. L., and J. R. Willis. 2004. Task-based instruction in foreign language education: Practices and program. Washington, DC: Georgetown University Press.

Lee, L. 2004. Learners' perspectives on networked collaborative interaction with native speakers of Spanish in the U.S. *Language, Learning & Technology* 8(1): 83–100. Retrieved July 20, 2006, from http://llt.msu.cdu/vol8num1/lee.

Leloup, J. W., and R. Ponterio. 2003. Interactive and multimedia techniques in online language lessons: A sampler. *Language Learning & Technology* 7(3): 4–17.

———. 2004. FLTEACH: On-line professional development preservice and inservice foreign language teachers. In *The Heinle professional series in language instruction.* Vol. 1, *Teaching with technology,* ed. L. Lomicka and J. Cooke-Plagwitz, 26–44. Boston: Heinle.

———. 2005. On the net: Vocabulary support for Independent online reading. *Language Learning & Technology* 9(2): 3–7. Retrieved August 30, 2006, from http://llt.msu.edu/vol9num2/net/default.html.

Lenhart, A., M. Madden, and P. Hitlin. 2005, July 27. Teens and technology: Youth are leading the transition to a fully wired and mobile nation. *Pew International & American Life Project.* Retrieved July 3, 2006, from www.pcwinternet.org/PPF/r/162/report_display.asp.

Levelt, W. 1989. *Speaking: From intention to articulation.* Cambridge, MA: MIT Press.

Levet, S., and S. Waryn, S. 2006. Using the web to develop students' in-depth understanding of foreign cultural attitudes and values. In *Changing language education through CALL,* ed. R. P. Donaldson and M. A. Haggstrom, 95–118. Abingdon: Routledge.

Levine, G., and S. Morse. 2004. Integrating diverse digital media in a global simulation German course. In *The Heinle professional series in language instruction.* Vol. 1, *Teaching with technology,* ed. L. Lomicka and J. Cooke-Plagwitz, 138–45. Boston: Heinle.

Levy, M. 1997. *Computer-assisted language learning: Context and conceptualisation.* Oxford, UK: Clarendon.

———. 2006. Effective use of CALL technologies: Finding the right balance. In *Changing language education through CALL,* ed. R. P. Donaldson and M. A. Haggstrom, 1–18. Abingdon: Routledge.

Levy, M., and G. Stockwell. 2006. *CALL dimensions: Options and issues in computer-assisted language learning.* Mahwah, NJ: Lawrence Erlbaum Associates.

Lightbrown, P. M., and N. Spada. 1993. *How languages are learned.* New York: Oxford University Press.

Lomicka, L. 2006. Understanding the other: Intercultural exchange and CMC. In *Calling on CALL: From theory and research to new directions in foreign language teaching,* ed. L. Ducate and N. Arnold, 211–36. CALICO Monograph Series, vol. 5. San Marcos, TX: CALICO.

Lomicka, L., and J. Cooke-Plagwitz, eds. 2004. *The Heinle professional series in language instruction: Vol. 1, Teaching with technology.* Boston, MA: Heinle.

Long, M., and P. Robinson. 1998. Focus on form: Theory, research, and practice. In *Focus on form in classroom second language acquisition,* ed. C. Doughty and J. Williams, 15–41. Cambridge: Cambridge University Press.

Long, M. H. 1981. Input, interaction and second language acquisition. In *Native language and foreign language acquisition,* ed. H. Winitz, 259–78. New York: Annals of the New York Academy of Science.

———. 1991. Focus on form: A design feature in language teaching methodology. In *Foreign language research in cross-cultural perspective,* ed. Claire Kramsch and Ralph Ginsberg, 39–52. Amsterdam: Benjamins.

MacWhinney, B. 1997. Implicit or explicit processes. *Studies in Second Language Acquisition* 19, 277–81.

Magnan, S. 2007. Reconsidering communicative language teaching for national goals. *Modern Language Journal* 91(2): 249–52.

Marton, F., and S. Booth, S. 1997. *Learning and awareness.* Mahwah, NJ: Lawrence Erlbaum Associates.

McGinnis, S. 1994. The less common alternative: A report from the Task Force for Teacher Training in the Less Commonly Taught Languages. *ADFL Bulletin* 25(2): 17–22.

McLaughlin, B. 1987. *Theories of second language learning.* London: Edward Arnold.

McLuhan, M. 1964. *Understanding media: The extension of man.* New York: Signet.

Meskill, C. 2005. Triadic scaffolds: Tools for teaching English language learners with computers. *Language Learning & Technology* 9(1): 46–59. Retrieved June 12, 2006, from http://llt.msu.edu/vol9num1/meskill/default.html.

Montrul, S. 2004. Subject and object expression in Spanish heritage speakers: A case of morpho-syntactic convergence. *Bilingualism: Language and Cognition* 7(2): 125–42.

Moore, J. 2004. *A synthesis of Sloan-C effective practices.* Retrieved May 15, 2007, from http://www.sloan-c.org/effective/.

Murray, G. L. 1999. Autonomy and language learning in a simulated environment. *System* 27, 295–308.

Murray, J., D. Morgenstern, and G. Furstenberg. 1989. The Athena Language Learning project: Design issues for the next generation of computer based language-learning tools. In *Modern technology in foreign language education: Applications and projects,* ed. W. F. Smith, 97–118. Lincolnwood, IL: National Textbook.

Nagata, N. 1993. Intelligent computer feedback for second language instruction. *Modern Language Journal* 77: 330–38.

———. 1995. An effective application of natural language processing in second language instruction. *CALICO Journal* 13(1): 47–67.

———. 1996. Computer vs. workbook instruction in second language acquisition. *CALICO Journal* 14(1): 53–75.

———. 2002. An application of natural language processing to web-based language learning. *CALICO Journal* 19(3): 583–99.

National Center for Educational Statistics. 2006. Enrollment in degree-granting institutions: Total enrollment. Retrieved August 31, 2007, from http://nces.ed.gov/programs/projections/sec2b.asp.

Nieves, K. A. 1996. The development of a technology-based class in beginning Spanish: Experiences with using *EXITO*. Unpublished PhD diss., George Mason University.

O'Dowd, R. 2003. Understanding "the other side": Intercultural learning in a Spanish-English e-mail exchange. *Language Learning and Technology* 7(2): 118–44.

———. 2005. Negotiating sociocultural and institutional contexts: The case of Spanish-American Telecollaboration. *Language and Intercultural Communication* 5(1): 40–56.

———. 2006. *Telecollaboration and the development of intercultural communicative competence.* Munich: Langenscheidt ELT GmbH.

O'Dowd, R., and M. Ritter. 2006. Understanding and working with "failed communication" in telecollaborative exchanges. *CALICO Journal* 23(3): 623–42.

O'Rourke, B. 2005. Form-focused interaction in online tandem learning. *CALICO Journal* 22(3): 433–66.

O'Rourke, B., and K. Schwienhorst. 2003. Talking text: Reflections on reflection in computer-mediated communication. In *Learner autonomy in foreign language teaching: Teacher, learner, curriculum, assessment,* ed. D. Little, J. Ridley, and E. Ushioda, 47–60. Dublin: Authentik.

Osuna, M. M., and C. Meskill, C. 1998. Using the world wide web to integrate Spanish language and culture: A pilot study. *Language Learning & Technology,* 1(2): 71–92. Retrieved June 12, 2006, from http://llt.msu.edu/vol1num2/article4/default.html.

Payne, S. 2004. Making the most of synchronous and asynchronous discussion in foreign language instruction. In *The Heinle professional series in language instruction. Vol. 1, Teaching with technology,* ed. L. Lomicka and J. Cooke-Plagwitz, 79–93. Boston: Heinle.

Payne, S., and P. J. Whitney. 2002. Developing L2 oral proficiency through synchronous CMC: Output, working memory and interlanguage development. *CALICO Journal* 20(1): 7–32.

Pedersen, K. M. 1987. Research on CALL. In *Modern media in foreign language education: Theory and implementation,* ed. W. Smith, 99–132. Lincolnwood, IL: National Textbook.

Pellettieri, J. 2000. Negotiation in cyberspace: The role of chatting in the development of grammatical competence. In *Network-based language teaching: Concepts and practice*, ed. M. Warschauer and R. Kern, 59–86. New York: Cambridge University Press.

Phillips, J. 1984. Practical implications of recent research in reading. *Foreign Language Annals* 17(4): 285–96.

Pica, T. 1994. Research on negotiation: What does it reveal about second-language learning conditions, processes, and outcomes? *Language Learning* 44: 493–527.

Pica, T., R. Kanagy, and J. Falodun. 1993. Choosing and using communication tasks for second language instruction. In *Tasks and language learning: Integrating theory and practice*, ed. G. Crookes and S. M. Gass, 9–34. Clevedon: Multilingual Matters.

Pinker, S. 1994[1995]. *The language instinct*. New York: W. Morrow and Co. and Harper Perennial.

Quinn, R. 1990. Our progress in integrating modern methods and computer-controlled learning for successful language study. *Hispania* 73(1): 297–311.

Reeves, B., and C. Nass. 1996. *The media equation: How people treat computers, television, and new media like real people and places*. Stanford, CA: CSLI Publications and Cambridge University Press.

Reynard, R. 2007, May 9. Instructional strategies for blogging. *Campus Technology*. Retrieved May 14, 2007, from www.campustechnology/article.aspx?aid = 47775.

Rheingold, H. 2000. *The virtual community*. Cambridge, MA: MIT Press. Retrieved May 24, 2006, from www.rheingold.com/vc/book/3.html.

Roblyer, M. D. 1988. The effectiveness of microcomputers in education: A review of research from 1980–87. *T.H.E. Journal* 16(2): 85–89.

Robb, T. N. 2006. Helping teachers to help themselves. In *Teacher education in CALL*, ed. P. Hubbard and M. Levy, 335–47. Language Learning & Language Teaching Series, vol. 14. Philadelphia: John Benjamin.

Russell, T. L. 2001. *The no significant difference phenomenon*, 5th ed. The International Distance Education Certification Center.

Salaberry, R. 1996. A theoretical foundation for the development of pedagogical tasks in computer mediated communication. *CALICO Journal* 14(1): 5–34.

———. 1997. "The role of input and output practice in second language acquisition." *The Canadian Modern Language Review/La Revue canadiene des langues vivantes*, 53(2): 422–51.

———. 2001. The use of technology for second language learning and teaching: A retrospective. *Modern Language Journal* 85(1): 39–56.

Schaumann, C., and A. Green. 2004. Enhancing the study of literature with the web. In *The Heinle professional series in language instruction*. Vol. 1, *Teaching with technology*, ed. L. Lomicka and J. Cooke-Plagwitz, 79–93. Boston: Heinle.

Schmidt, R. W. 1990. The role of consciousness in second language acquisition. *Applied Linguistics* 11(2): 219–58.

Schmidt, R. W., and S. N. Frota. 1986. Developing basic conversational ability in a second language: A case study of an adult learner of Portuguese. In *Talking to learn: Conversation in second language acquisition*, ed. R. R. Day, 237–326. Rowley, MA: Newbury House.

Schulze, M. 2001. Human language technologies in computer-assisted language learning. In *ICT and language learning: A European perspective*, ed. A. Chambers and G. Davies, 111–32. Lisse: Sets and Zeitlinger.

Scida, E., and R. E. Saury. 2006. Hybrid courses and their impact on student and classroom performance: A case study at the University of Virginia. *CALICO Journal* 23(3): 517–31.

Selber, S. A. 2004. *Multiliteracies for a digital age*. Carbondale: Southern Illinois University Press.

Skehan, P. 1989. *Individual differences in second-language learning*. London: Arnold.

Smith, Bryan. 2003. Computer-mediated negotiated interaction: An expanded model. *Modern Language Journal* 87(1): 38–54.

Soo, K., and Y. Ngeow. 1998. Effective English as a second language (ESL) instruction with interactive multimedia: The MCALL project. *Journal of Educational Multimedia and Hypermedia* 7(1): 71–89.

Sotillo, S. M. 2000. Discourse functions and syntactic complexity in synchronous and asynchronous communication. *Language Learning & Technology* 4(1): 82–119. Retrieved December 10, 2006, from http://llt.msu.edu/vol4num1/sotillo/default .html.

Stryker, S. B., and B. L. Leaver, eds. 1997. *Content-based instruction in foreign language education: Models and methods*. Washington, DC: Georgetown University Press.

Swaffar, J. 1998. Networking language learning: introduction. In *Language learning online: Theory and practice in the ESL and L2 computer classroom*, ed. J. Swaffar, S. Romano, P. Markley, and K. Arens, 1–15. Austin, TX: Labyrinth Publications.

Swain, M. 1985. Communicative competence: some roles of comprehensible input and comprehensible output in its development. In *Input in second language acquisition*, ed. C. Madden and S. M. Gass, 235–53. Rowley, MA: Newbury House.

———. 2000. The output hypothesis and beyond: Mediating acquisition through collaborative dialogue. In *Sociocultural theory and second language learning*, ed. J. P. Lantolf, 97–114. Oxford: Oxford University Press.

Terrell, T. D., M. Andrade, J. Egasse, and M. Muñoz. 2002. *Dos mundos*. New York: McGraw-Hill.

Thompson, I., and D. Hiple. 2005. Preface. In *Selected papers from the 2004 NFLRC symposium: Distance education, distributed learning and language instruction (NetWork#44)*, ed. I. Thompson and D. Hiple. [HTML document]. Honolulu: University of Hawai'i, National Foreign Language Resource Center. Retrieved March 6, 2006, from http://nflrc.hawaii.edu/NetWorks/NW44.

Thorne, S. L. 2003. Artifacts and cultures-of-use in intercultural communication. *Language Learning & Technology* 7(2): 38–67. Retrieved July 18, 2006, from http://llt.msu.edu/vol7num2/thorne/.

Thorne, S. L., and J. S. Payne. 2005. Evolutionary trajectories, Internet-mediated expression, and language education. *CALICO Journal* 22(3): 371–97.

Turing, A. 1950. Computing machinery and intelligence. *Mind*, new series 59(236):

433–60. Retrieved August 30, 2006, from http://cogprints.org/499/00/turing.html.

Underwood, J. 1984. *Linguistics, computers, and the language teacher.* Rowley, MA: Newbury House.

———. 1989. On the edge: Intelligent CALL in the 1990s. *Computers and the Humanities* 23(1): 71–84.

Ushida, E. 2007. Robo-Sensei Personal Japanese Tutor, version 1.0. *CALICO Journal,* 24(2): 408–20.

Van de Pol, J. 2001. *Spanish without walls: Using technology to teach language anywhere.* Retrieved April 16, 2008, from http://ittimes.ucdavis.edu/mar2001/blake.html

van Dijk, J. A. G. M. 2005. *The deepening divide: Inequality in the information society.* London: Sage.

VanPatten, B. 1996. *Input processing and grammar instruction: Theory and research.* Norwood, NJ: Ablex.

Varonis, E. M., and S. M. Gass. 1985. Non-native/non-native conversations: A model for negotiation of meaning. *Applied Linguistics* 6(1): 71–90.

Vogel, T. 2001. Learning out of control: Some thoughts on the world wide web in learning and teaching foreign languages. In *ICT and language learning: A European perspective,* ed. A. Chambers and G. Davies, 135–45. Lisse: Swets and Zeitlinger.

Vygotsky, L. 1962. *Thought and language.* Cambridge, MA: MIT Press.

Walczynski, S. 2002. Applying the job characteristics model to Mallard web-based classes. Unpublished PhD diss., Illinois State University.

Ware, P. D., and C. Kramsch, C. 2005. Toward an intercultural stance: Teaching German and English through telecollaboration. *Modern Language Journal* 89(2): 190–205.

Warschauer, M. 1995. *Virtual connections.* Honolulu, HI: Second Language Teaching & Curriculum Center, University of Hawai'i at M&amacr$noa.

———. 1997a. Computer-mediated collaborative learning. *Modern Language Journal* 81(4): 470–81.

———. 1997b. Comparing face-to-face and electronic discussion in the second language classroom. *CALICO Journal* 13(2–3): 7–26.

———. 2002. Reconceptualizing the digital divide. *First Monday* 7(7). Retrieved June 30, 2006, from http://firstmonday.org/issues/issue7_7/warschauer/index.html.

———. 2004. Technological change and the future of CALL. In *New perspectives on CALL for second and foreign language classrooms,* ed. S. Fotos and C. Brown, 15–25). Mahwah, NJ: Lawrence Erlbaum Associates.

Warschauer, M., and I. De Florio-Hansen. 2003. Multilingualism, identity, and the Internet. In *Multiple identity and multilingualism,* ed. A. Hu and I. De Florio-Hansen, 155–79. Tübingen: Stauffenburg.

Warschauer, M., M. Knobel, and L. Stone. 2004. Technology and equity in schooling: Deconstructing the digital divide. *Educational Policy* 18(4): 562–88.

Warschauer, M., L. Turbee, and B. Roberts. 1996. Computer learning networks and student empowerment. *System* 24: 1–14.

Weizenbaum, J. 1966. ELIZA—A computer program for the study of natural language communication between man and machine [electronic version]. *Communications of the ACM* 9(1): 35–36. Retrieved January 11, 2007, from http://i5.nyu.edu/~mm64/x52.9265/january1966.html.

Wildner-Bassett, M. E. 2005. CMC as written conversation: A critical social-constructivist view of multiple identities and cultural positioning in the L2/C2 classroom. *CALICO Journal* 22(3): 635–56.

Wiley, T. 2007. Heritage and community languages in the national language debate: Beyond xenophobia and national security as bases for U.S. policy. *Modern Language Journal* 91(2): 252–55.

Winke, P., and D. MacGregor. 2001. Review of *Hot Potatoes*. *Language Learning & Technology* 5(2): 28–33. Retrieved September 1, 2006, at http://llt.msu.edu/vol5num2/review3/default.htm.

Young, J. 2002. Hybrid teaching seeks to end the divide between traditional and online instruction. *Chronicle of Higher Education* 48(28): A33.

Zhao, Y., M. J. Alvarez-Torres, B. Smith, and H. S. Tan. 2005. The non-neutrality of technology: A theoretical analysis and empirical study of computer mediated communication technologies. In *Research in technology and second language learning: Developments and directions*, ed. Y. Zhao, 281–316. Greenwich, CT: Information Age.

Index

Note: Italicized page numbers followed by *t* or *f* represent tables and figures in the text.

173